'DEAD RES

OR

THE TECHNIQUES OF

GUIDING

LOST SOULS

by Michael Evans

CON-PSY PUBLICATIONS

First Edition

© Michael Evans
2007

This book is copyrighted under the Berne Convention. All rights reserved. No part of this book may be reproduced or utilised in any form or by any means, electronic or mechanical, including photocopying, recording, or by any information storage and retrieval system, without permission in writing from the publisher. Except for the purpose of reviewing or criticism, as permitted under the Copyright Act of 1956.

Published by

CON-PSY PUBLICATIONS

P.O. BOX 14,
GREENFORD,
MIDDLESEX, UB6 0UF.

ISBN 978 1 898680 45 1

CONTENTS

PART 1 THE PREPARATION — **Page**
Chapter 1 THE SCEPTIC MEETS THE SPIRITUAL. — 7
    The Voice in the Cathedral. Taught by the Brotherhood
Chapter 2 PAST LIVES. Nancy Passing and Return. — 15
    The Brotherhood and the Tapes
Chapter 3 HEAVENLY MATCHMAKERS. A Marriage. — 25

PART II THE RESCUES BEGIN
Chapter 4 THE FIRST GULF WAR. Those Who Die in Battle. — 33
    Juanita is helped. Four Teenagers.
    A South African Rescue. Mark the Skier meets his Mother.
Chapter 5 SOME DIFFICULT RESCUES — 43
    An Awkward Customer. Mr McKintyre's Trouble.
    Wilf in the Dark Regions.
    A Welsh Lady is Puzzled. The Girl in Her Coffin.
    Billy Does Not Think He Is Dead.
Chapter 6 MORE CASES. Walking, Walking, Walking. — 60
    A Teenager in Pain. Hanged By The Neck.
    A Victorian Awake. A Scientist Returns to Teach Us..
Chapter 7 DO WE ALWAYS SUCCEED? — 71
    A Catholic Priest in Distress. A Flirtatious Spirit.
    Letitia- So Selfish
    Unable to Help. The Group Changes.
Chapter 8 DO RELIGIOUS BELIEFS HELP AFTER DEATH? — 82
    Helping A Nun. Helping a Salvationist. Helping A Muslim.
    What a Churchman Finds. High Churchmen in the Afterlife.
Chapter 9 THE SECOND GULF WAR — 96
    Bombed in Baghdad. An Iraqi is helped.
    The role of the Grandmother. The War in Sri Lanka.
Chapter 10 ANIMALS TO THE RESCUE — 102
    Two dogs come to help. Donkeys help. A Cat helps.
    Freddie can't get home but a dog helps.
Chapter 11 WHO ELSE DOES RESCUE WORK? — 110
    The Rev. Roberts. The SRF Foundation.
    Exorcists in the Churches. Rescues in other cultures.
    CONFESSION IS GOOD FOR THE SOUL
    Jack confesses. Helmut, a Nazi confesses. Sandra confesses.
Chapter 12 INTERESTING VISITORS — 121
    A London Gang Leader. A Lady of the Night.
    9/11 The Twin Towers The language problem.

	Page
PART III THE HAUNTINGS	
Chapter 13 GHOST BUSTING OR SPIRIT RELEASE?	131

Our First Haunting. The Haunted Flat The Ghost at KFC.
A Mischievous Ghost haunts ten houses.
A Disturbing Entity and a Romantic Outcome.

Chapter 14 DESPERATE APPEALS.   142

Driven from home. A Doctor asks for help.
Two ghosts and a suicide.
Testimony. Haunted for nine years.

Chapter 15 WHAT DO PEOPLE DO IN THE SPIRIT WORLD?   160

A Bank Manager tell' his story. Children in the Spirit World.
Is there any proof? What does Science say? A Poem..
CONCLUSION What do people need to know?
The Curse of Ignorance. What to teach children?

FURTHER READING.   169

Dedicated to;
Colin Fry, John Edward and James Van Praagh who, by their TV programs and books, have demonstrated to tens of millions of viewers around the world, that mediums can facilitate communication with people in the life following this one.

And to trance mediums
Katherine, Sheila, Judy, Jean, Valerie, John and Ronald, And sitters John, Suzanne, Lily, Joy and Jack who have freely given of their time and gifts to rescue distressed Spirits from the situations described in this book.

'DEAD RESCUE'

Space telescopes, and electronic microscopes, have shown us things in nature, which we knew nothing about.

Talking to the dead shows us things that were unknown to science or religion. Reading this book will show how and why Rescue Work is carried out. Not everyone can do this work - but everyone can learn why some people NEED to be rescued - and this knowledge can safeguard them and those they love from suffering a similar fate after death!*

*After death Sir Arthur Conan Doyle sent back a message: "We have before us a mighty work. We must spread the truth so that souls do not come over here to dwell in darkness."

'DEAD RESCUE' or
THE TECHNIQUES OF GUIDING LOST SOULS
PART 1   THE PREPARATION
CHAPTER 1

The Skeptic meets the Spiritual

Had I seen the title of this book when I was 18, I would have scoffed at it. What a ridiculous idea! How can you rescue someone who does not exist? I felt that the dead were dead, gone, obliterated. How could they be rescued?

I believed then in science, logic and evidence. Tales of an afterlife, I thought, were mere fairy tales, handed down to us by our unscientific, credulous, ancestors When, serving in the RAF, I was bombed and shot at, I had little fear of death, although I was certainly afraid of injury, for to me death meant oblivion. .

I still believe in logic, science and evidence. How did it come about then that I found myself actively engaged in talking to, and helping to rescue, more than two hundred and seventy individuals and groups who had passed through the gate of death and ended up in a distressing situation, from which they were unable to escape without help. Most were brought to our circle to be helped, but to deal with others we had to visit haunted houses and sites where people were troubled by trapped, and sometimes malevolent entities. I was to undergo a long period of training and many experiences before I could be useful in this way.

Although I declared myself an atheist when young, and even objected to attending morning assembly at school, because it was a religious ceremony, there was always, at the back of my mind, a feeling that there might be something else besides this physical world. I think I was about three years old when my mother took me on a coach trip. I was standing up on the seat, looking out of the window at a wonderful sunset, when a lovely feeling swept over me that my real home was somewhere out there. I knew my mother was clever and beautiful but I also knew I could not tell her about this, because she would not understand.

In my adolescence, this gradually faded from my memory. In school I loved science, the only subject in which I shone. For me, science, not religion, held the truth about the universe.

The Voice in the Cathedral

In the RAF, I maintained my public scepticism about a spiritual world beyond this one, and enjoyed debating the subject with a friend who was a monk prior to joining up. However a shock awaited me. I had been to

London to collect my new RAF officer's uniform from a tailor in London's West End, and I caught a train to the West Country, where I planned to meet my fiancée - later to become my wife. My train stopped at Salisbury and we were told there would not be one on to Devon for two hours.

To pass the time, I wandered into Salisbury Cathedral. As I walked towards the East Window I remember thinking that when they erected this building, they really believed that one could communicate with the Divine. As I neared the altar, three separate things happened to me.

Firstly, I felt an overwhelming desire to throw myself on the floor with my arms spread out in the form of a cross. It was as if a giant magnet had been switched on to pull me down. The floor was dusty and I had my precious brand new uniform on, and I succeeded in staying upright, by struggling against the downward pull. Next I went blind; all ahead was black, and high up in the darkness, I saw a brilliant golden circle of light surrounded by deep blue. In the golden light I saw a face while at the same time a great voice pealed out like an organ, the two words, "LOVE THEM!" I remember nothing after this until my sight returned, when I found I had moved about fifty feet away down a side aisle. I was now surrounded by a small group of people who were looking at me with wondering concern. I don't know what I looked like. As I looked at them, I was amazed to see that they were all glowing with an internal light, and into my mind came the word, "Angels?"

As I came to, I found that I still had my Air Force hat under my arm, and I wandered out into the spring sunshine, full of wonder. "Who had spoken to me? And why? It was to be a life long quest.

After this incident, my interest in the spiritual, and inner life was aroused and my subsequent research led me through Buddhism, Gospel Churches, and confirmation in the Church of England and on to the Quakers. From the start, my wife had joined me in the search, and we might well have stayed with the Quakers but another shock awaited me.

A Spiritual Healing

I was doing up an old house for my daughter, when I started to move a heavy three-stage wooden ladder, with a bucket of cement on the top. I felt something give at the top of my spine and soon I was in great pain in both arms and both legs. I was unable to go to my job as a head of department at a large comprehensive school and my doctor and the local orthopaedic hospital could not cure the trouble. The only way to stop the pain was to sit bolt upright. I sat on a settee, night and day, for five weeks with no improvement. In desperation my wife suggested that we went to the

Exeter Spiritualist Church, where an advertisement said there would be Spiritual Healing after the service.

I did not really want to go, but my wife persuaded me. I could still drive if I sat upright, and we went to the nicely decorated modern church and sat right at the back. I was completely healed in a ten-minute session at the end of the service and the problem has never returned.

To me, the Spiritualist service, and the messages passed to people in the congregation were interesting but incredible! I thought these people can't be so gullible as to think that the dead can communicate. However, I took the trouble to investigate in some detail, the message received by a lady on my left from her three-year old deceased daughter. She confirmed every detail of the message, had just moved to Exeter, and had never been to a Spiritualist Church before. I could find no way of explaining it away as trickery.

This occurred in October 1977. My wife and I began to attend the church regularly, and soon a series of convincing messages were given to us from relatives and close friends we had thought 'dead'. My father, a Cambridge mathematician, said,

'I would not have had this in the house, but I find it to be true.'

By 'chance', at this time, I was asked to take charge of religious education for six hundred of the older pupils at the school where I taught, and I was able to introduce a course on "Life after Death" which became the most popular subject I had ever taught in school. Pupils would ask in other lessons, "Can't we talk about Life After Death? That's interesting!"

A Meditation Group

On the twelfth of March 1978, a visiting medium to the church told us that we should be joining a meditation circle. A similar message came to another church member shortly afterwards, and at intervals, the same message came to others. On the fourteenth of September 1979, our circle gathered for the first time for meditation and the discussion of spiritual topics.

As we continued with our weekly meditations, one member, Harry Smith, an ex-merchant seaman, began to fall into trance. When he awoke, he described being with teachers in white monks' robes, who told him that he would be a healer and no harm would come to any of us. At this stage, we felt the need of an experienced teacher of meditation who could explain what was happening to us. We were fortunate in that a well-known medium, George Pratt, and his wife Louise, joined us and we made steady progress under his teachings.

Taught by the Brotherhood

It was on the twelfth of September 1980 that, to our surprise, George Pratt. in meditation, was transfigured by another face appearing over his, while an august and noble voice spoke through him saying:

"We have long sought you. It is very difficult for man's finite mind to appreciate the infinite. Truth enlarges as man progresses ... My brothers call me White Ray. I will come again."

When we told George what had happened to him, he explained that many years before, the White Brotherhood, especially one called The Tibetan, had regularly taught through him, and he was delighted to think that he would be used again for this purpose.

The circle then began to have regular visitations from members of the White Brotherhood, speaking through George, and we recorded, and transcribed, hundreds of pages of guidance and instruction. These will not form part of this book but our visitors were exquisitely polite as this example from the Tibetan indicates:

"It is the Tibetan who speaks. With what affection are we able to approach you. With what hope within us do we look upon you and hear your own teachings of each other, whenever you meet together. When first I heard your comments and your discussion, I came with more than a little trepidation, for it seems as if you have said all, in the comments which are offered around your group. But it may be that I may be able to enlarge, perhaps a little, on some of the things which you have said."

White Ray too could be extraordinarily courteous in speaking to a very ordinary group of people, when speaking through George: He said,

"My beloveds! Because of your accumulated efforts in meditation, you present as an oasis in the midst of a vast and empty desert - I who am known as White Ray am able to be present with you for a short time, and greet you with the joy of supreme consciousness. We of the White Brothers welcome you, as we hope, and always pray, that you will welcome us. I wonder if you are truly aware of the consciousness we call the White Brotherhood. It comprises much of those of past civilisations. It comprises, also, much of the experiences of other planetary influences, making a vast wealth of understanding, through the experience of universal life. You surely must be aware that it is more than mere fantasy, and that necessarily it is more than the confines of the stone on which you stand, your Earth!"

The doubt as to whether all this could be fantasy came to us occasionally, and the Tibetan arranged a demonstration to show the reality of his power. He asked my wife to take the medium's pulse and, while we waited, he stopped the pulse. George's wife was in the group! My mind conjured up the headlines in the papers if the pulse did not start again. After what seemed an age, my wife said, "It has started!" We breathed a sigh of relief - and belief.

In the early days, the Tibetan mentioned our having come together through Spiritualism, he said:

"You have, through a number of schools of thought, entered that which is known among you as Spiritualism, and this has contributed greatly to a furtherance of your knowledge; yet it is not intended that this 'ism', as such, shall contain your entirety, for there is much to be disclosed, much yet to be understood."

He also said that while we had a 'rendezvous' to meet in this life, we were only at the beginning of our progress. He named us the Alpha Group, and made it clear that there was a great deal of preparatory work to be done in laying the foundations of our spiritual training. We were told that each of us would reach a point where a decision would have to be made. In his words:

"Your journey will take you to that which may be called the crossroads, and here is where your decision is made. If you decide to retrace your steps from this point, you are not held in any way in disrespect, for it is well known that man, the lower self, is but a child. But if you have grown to adulthood at the time you reach the crossroads, and you decide to go on, you will realise then, that this is the point of no return, and your life will then be devoted to the service of God - knowing that God is life, and understanding this simple yet complex statement."

The Brothers who came to teach us, appeared to be part of a vast group-mind and had no personal egotism. They were not at all anxious to be named, but they realised that we felt a need to know who was speaking to us. I often wondered if our Tibetan was THE Tibetan who co-operated with Alice Bailey in writing the classic series of books, published by the Lucis Trust between 1919 and 1949. It was several years before he mentioned that it was he who worked with Alice Bailey and Madam Blavatsky.

I found that the Lucis Trust had offices in the United Nations Building in New York, and 3 Whitehall Court, Suite 54, London SW1A 2EF. When I obtained copies of the books he had dictated, such as, 'The Externalisation of the Hierarchy,' and 'A Treatise on Cosmic Fire,' I soon realised that the vast understanding and knowledge displayed in them was too great for the limited capacity of my memory. I could get incredible vistas of knowledge from them but I could not retain them, and the teachings we were receiving in the Alpha Group were better adjusted to our capacity to grasp them.

A book I particularly wanted was the Tibetan's, 'Discipleship in the New Age', but at the time I did not feel justified in spending the money on it. Then, one evening, as I was standing by the library cupboard in the Spiritualist Church, a young man walked in, came directly to me and said this is for you. It was a copy of the very book I wanted. "Who are you?" I said, "Please write your name in it!" He wrote, 'A Solar!' And left... I never saw him again.

Usually the Tibetan's talk would end with "Is there that that you would ask me?" Once I asked if there would be changes on the Earth in the near future. He answered quite sharply, "Changes? Political? Economic? What do you mean?
Self: "Spiritual."
Tibetan: "My friend, you have yet to know a traumatic time before such a situation can come about ... By that I do not think in terms of the destruction which some of your fellows appear to be concerned with (nuclear war)... But prepare for a time round about the end of your present century, when many of your people will turn, alas, from desperation, to things spiritual. This is why at this time we strive to inspire such as you to prepare. It is as though you were those in the forefront of the battle, prepared and waiting for the casualties, that you may tend their wounds. Be of good cheer, be of good faith, for you will be needed."
I had no idea what this could involve at the time

By now Harry's gift of healing was well established. When my sister, who had an old ski-ing injury, could get no help from Harley Street, I invited her to Exeter, and Harry's gift successfully cured what medical science had failed to alleviate.

We had an interesting confirmation of our teachings in the group, on one of the rare occasions when we were all together at a service in the Exeter Spiritualist Church. The visiting medium, a Mr.Donelly, picked us out, although we were not all sitting together. Amongst other things, he said, "For all of you, the search is now over, take your time. In your group, keep sitting. The Master will come. Listen to the voice. Put it on tape. You have all known each other before. You had to come back. You will meet with majesty."

The 'majesty' mentioned here, turned out to be one of several visitors who overshadowed George, and spoke to us occasionally. Three times, Rameses II of Egypt, has come to our circle, as had Alfred Russell Wallace, the co-originator of the theory of evolution with Darwin, and once, Winston Churchill. Winston's voice was unmistakable. He said this was the first time he had been able to communicate, and that the chaotic leaders of a nation would cause a problem 'in a five' – but all would be well in the end. This meant nothing to us, but five months later the Argentine Junta launched an attack on the Falkland Islands and Britain was at war with

Argentina, which ended with the freeing of the islands from foreign occupation.

When Rameses II visited, George was transfigured, and we all saw the elaborate Egyptian Costume and headdress complete with snake's head projecting from it, but my wife, ever the truth seeker, was not satisfied until we found a picture of Rameses' actual death mask; then we all agreed that this was the man whose face we had seen over George's face.

The Brothers said,

"It is essential that a foothold, as it were, shall be gained among mankind, for his sight is blinded by the glitter of his folly, and because he is so dazzled, he cannot see or recognise the guiding hand which is offered. Thus do we call you together who came for this purpose."

One day, when we meditated, a voice of truly awesome magnificence and authority spoke through George. I reproduce here the relevant portions of the words we heard:

"I am told that in your conversation this evening, you spoke of a crisis year. To some extent, this is so. It is also true that because it is a crisis year, it does not follow that disaster will be the result. The life force moves in ebb and flow, and this you already realise. That which you spoke of as a crisis time will be the time of a low ebb.

It is the folly of man which makes these disasters at these times. The time is on the ebb and from that the flow will emerge in full blossom, when great benefits are experienced.

As far as you are able, Love, for this is the force, this is the undeniable power, which underlies all things. First there was Love and last there will be Love: the power which will enable you to speak to your cousins, and to all things about you, which can enable you to touch and it will be so. This must be your target.

You will hear some things in your crisis year, which may appear to be inglorious, which may appear to be tragic. You will know even the overthrow of Governments. You will know natural catastrophes, but wait - from the ebb to the flow. You are power within yourselves, my friends, a force for good, which even now can have an effect. Direct it to those in need, individually and collectively; but be together, together!'

We were familiar with the voices of several of our teachers as they spoke through George Pratt, but this voice was more powerful than any we had heard before. One if us must have wondered who the speaker was. After an interval, it continued, even louder than before,

"Even now you ask 'Who is this? Feel! Know! Accept!

I am the breath in the morning,

I am the lull in the night.

I am that which comes as I said I would come,

And I will be known by those who know me,
And I will not be known by strangers,
Yet that which I give, I must give to all.
I am the dawn and the sunset,
I am the sun and the stars,
I am love!"

The feeling engendered among us by this beautiful voice can hardly be expressed in words.

PAST LIVES
CHAPTER 2

It was during this time that my wife, Nancy, and I, listened to a radio programme, 'The Bloxham Tapes', on the BBC. Arnold Bloxham was a man who could not become a medical doctor because of an earlier infection, but instead became a hypnotherapist. He had many memories of his own past lives and had actually visited places he had lived in, in those past lives. In trying to heal a man who had an overwhelming fear of death he attempted to regress him into a memory of a previous life, to show him that he had lived before, and therefore death was not the end. The patient at once reverted into a previous life where he had had another wife and family in another century. Having discovered the technique, Arnold experimented for many years, with the patients' permission, and regressed many hundreds of people into memories of previous lives. On the BBC programme, he asked back people who had been regressed previously, and regressed them again in the studio. We listened to the programme, and the two repeats, and decided to investigate it ourselves.

At that time a man called Barney Camfield was running a course in Plymouth called Psycho-expansion. It was not claimed to be regression but was designed to give people the actual feeling of being another person at another time. Whether this proved the truth of reincarnation was a matter for each individual to decide.

My wife and I were invited to attend a Thursday evening in Plymouth, when an advanced group met. They had, we were told, shown the ability to experience other lives and were capable of leading their own groups. We were warmly greeted and Barney set a little test to see if the members were able to describe the house we lived in. As we were completely unknown to the group and had come forty miles to the meeting, it was an intriguing idea - especially as we lived at that time in such an unusual house. Most of the descriptions were far from the truth, describing very conventional houses, but one lady was extremely accurate, including the fact that the garden was on the other side of the road, was entered through a green door and overlooked a large river. When I questioned her later, she said she could sit in her kitchen, go into a light trance, and watch her twelve - year old daughter as she went into town, to make sure she was safe.

We watched the session as Barney went through a simple relaxation routine and members were told to go to any date that interested them. They were told they could return to the present at any time if they encountered anything distressing. After only six minutes they were told to return and write down their experiences. It took about twenty minutes for them all to finish writing and then each in turn read what they had written unless, they preferred to 'pass'.

The first lady said she had gone back to her own eighth birthday. She had been given a ten shilling National Savings Certificate as her only present and was allowed to have the girl next door to tea as a treat. For celebration there was a rare thing, a plate of fancy iced biscuits on the table, and she had set her heart on the one in the centre, which had a brown and white design. Her mother told her to offer the plate to the visitor, who naturally took the very biscuit she had set her heart on. She burst into tears at this and was sent to bed for her bad behaviour.

The next lady said she knew the end of her 18th century Dutch life, when she had drowned when the ship carrying her to the New World had foundered in a gale. She now wanted to experience her earlier life in Holland, and had found herself holding her mother's hand as they walked along the side of a canal. They both carried fish baskets and she was dressed in clothes which were a smaller edition of her mother's. They watched the barges going to and fro as they walked towards the fish market. There were six other detailed accounts and Nancy and I resolved to return and take part in the sessions and experience these things for ourselves.

I was not very successful, perhaps because I was so anxious not to imagine something, and so deceive myself. My most vivid, and quite unexpected experience, came when I found myself a girl of about twelve years of age, wearing my best frock with puffed sleeves, looking out of the window of the front parlour of a farmhouse. I was watching the men working in my father's fields and wondered if they were kind to their little girls. I thought I don't know any men except my father. I knew that the passage outside the door had a cobbled floor and ran from the front door to the kitchen.

Nancy, on the other hand, was extremely successful and experienced lives totally at odds with her own. In one life she found herself a male Eskimo in a kayak, cooperating with others in driving a group of seals on to the shore in order to kill them. In another, she found herself a male again, a gamekeeper, who enjoyed shooting any predators who threatened his pheasants. This was startling to a woman who was a devoted animal lover. In another, as female, she felt her head was of a very different shape and her hair was dark, greasy, long and tangled. She was watching a religious procession and knew she was in Tibet.

After some weeks of this, when we were sitting in the group with George Pratt, the Tibetan said in a rather disapproving way, "Some of you have even tried to find out who you were in past lives. This is not necessary!" As a result we withdrew from the Psycho-expansion group but we could not forget what we had experienced and did return to it some years later and met several people who were to become members of our rescue group at a later date. On one evening, Barney was unable to come and he phoned, and asked me to take over. To my surprise I was able to regress people as effectively as Barney but then he had already trained them and I simply followed his pattern.

At this stage I can well imagine my reader (or myself at eighteen) saying this is all very wonderful and fantastic, but can we believe it? Is the writer a trustworthy witness? Did all this really happen?

After nineteen years as a magistrate, sitting on hundreds of cases, I know the difficulty of deciding whether a witness is telling the truth. In my defence, let me say that nearly all that took place was recorded on audio tape, and the rescues which will be described later on, were also recorded, and I still have the tapes filed away. Apart from that I can only put my life's pattern forward and leave the readers to judge whether I am likely to be a reliable witness. The book is not about me but about the people we have been able to help so I will make it brief.I volunteered for the RAF, aged nineteen years, when this country was expecting to be invaded by the hugely successful German armed forces, and the Battle of Britain was about to begin. Unable, like my friends, to go for aircrew because of my eyesight, I became a ground gunner and fired many thousands of rounds at attacking German aircraft. Eventually I became the Flight Sergeant in number 2751 Squadron of the newly formed RAF Regiment, before going as a staff instructor to the RAF Officer Cadet Training Unit in the Isle of Man.

When I was commissioned as an officer, I changed to the Flying Control branch of the RAF, serving at many aerodromes in the UK, India and Burma. I ended up as Senior Flying Control Officer at RAF Station, Lahore, in India (now Pakistan), before returning to the UK to train as a teacher. In time I became a Head of Department and acted for a time, as Head of the Lower School of six hundred pupils. By now I had been asked to become a magistrate and was chairman of various local bodies and secretary of a local Spiritualist Church. I am not particularly clever compared to other members of my family but many people have been kind enough to trust me with various matters and I can only hope that my readers will do the same and accept that my account is as accurate as I can make it.

NANCY'S PASSING AND RETURN
Let me not, to the marriage of true minds,
Admit impediment. Love is not love
That alters where it alteration finds.

William Shakespeare Sonnet 116

If you are romantic, you may enjoy this chapter. If you only want to read about rescuing the dead, you may prefer to skip this chapter and read on.

My wife, Nancy, had had paratyphoid when young, which held her back from playing games for a time, but when we met in our twenties, she was very fit, keeping up with me easily on long walks over the moors, although I was in regular training in the RAF Regiment. In her sixties her heart trouble gradually returned but she never gave in. She insisted on cooking lunch on the day she passed. At 9 p.m. that evening, she said, "I've had enough! I want to be out of my body!" She passed during the night.

The day before, she had said to her grandson, "If I die, Tim, I'm going to sort out this communication business".

We had been happily married for 45 years and no one escapes grief when a loved one dies: the empty chair, the empty bed, the empty house; all shout the loved ones absence. Even the dog is grieving. We had been used to getting messages from people who had passed on, either in Spiritualist Churches, or from our many friends who were mediums, but the big question in my mind was 'Would Nancy be able to come through to say she was all right?'

I had no idea what a brilliant communicator she would prove to be. I will only quote a few of the hundreds of messages I received from her, and still receive to this day. I've put them in capital letters, to try to show the impact they had on me at the time, and the effect they had on my later life. Within 36 hours of her passing, Nancy came through to Sheila, one of the members of our meditation group, as she was coming out of the shower. She was asked to tell me:

"DON'T FORGET THE PRESENTS FOR THE GRANDCHILDREN IN THE TOP CUPBOARD IN THE LIVING ROOM, AND, IF LITTLE KATHLEEN IS CRYING, GIVE HER THE LITTLE LEATHER BAG OF FAMILY JEWELLERY TO PLAY WITH, WHICH IS IN THE DRAWER BY THE HATCH."

Later that day, Kathleen came to the house, went straight to the drawer, took out the leather bag and started to play with the bits of jewellery. Her mother said she had been crying for several hours.

The following day I went to the service at the Exeter Spiritualist Church where I was now secretary. The medium was a new one to Exeter, Barbara Kear-Morgan. She came to me with a message:

"I HAVE A LOVELY LADY HERE WHO THOUGHT OF EVERYONE BEFORE HERSELF. SHE WANTED TO DO SO MUCH MORE, BUT WAS TOLD SHE MUST STOP AND HAVE REST AND PEACE. SHE SAYS THE SAME APPLIES TO YOU. YOU MUST HAVE

SOME REST AND PEACE. SHE SENDS DEEP LOVE."

The following day, a Sunday, I went to the church service again, but this time my friend, the medium, Sheila, came with me. I was given another message about my work now continuing, but it was not from Nancy. To my surprise, Sheila looked as though something was delighting her. I asked her,

'Why the smiles?" and she said that Nancy was sitting next to her during the service and, "She said to me that you would get the next message but one - and you did - and she said you have two pairs of socks on."

This remark amazed me! I had spent the morning, doing what Nancy had asked, which was to put all her clothes into black plastic sacks, so that they could go to a centre collecting clothes for refuges abroad. I had come across a new pair of long socks, still in the original packet, and, as it was a very cold day, I had put them on over my short socks, which were now invisible. My heart leapt at the thought that she had been there, watching me as I worked, when I thought I was alone in the house.

A few days later, my psychic friend, Katherine, rang from a hospital bed, where she was recovering from, an operation. She said,

"NANCY HAS BEEN HERE. SHE IS WORRIED THAT YOU STILL HAVE NOT FOUND SOMETHING IMPORTANT".

A week later, a visitor discovered some more wrapped Christmas presents, hidden, at the back of the larder. I realised that Nancy had not been well enough to climb up and put them back in the top cupboard, after wrapping them.

On the 4th December, Valerie, a very sensitive group member, was in bed when she heard Nancy's voice quite distinctly. It said;

"HELLO VALERIE! HOW ARE YOU? THERE'S REALLY NOTHING TO WORRY ABOUT YOU KNOW. IT WAS SO EASY! I JUST SORT OF SLIPPED OUT. I WAS SURROUNDED BY ALL THIS BEAUTIFUL GREEN. YOU KNOW HOW I LIKED THAT COLOUR. I'M REALLY QUITE LOOKING FORWARD TO THURSDAY."

Thursday, 7th December, was to be the day of the funeral, when she would see many friends and family gathered together. At the funeral, during the address, Valerie again heard Nancy's voice saying;

"HELLO VALERIE! I'M GLAD YOU COULD COME."

During the singing of the 23rd Psalm, Valerie heard Nancy's voice again, saying,

"ISN'T IT FUNNY! HERE I AM, AND HALF THE PEOPLE DON'T EVEN KNOW IT".

She sounded so bright and cheery that Valerie nearly laughed out loud.

Later, I was told that Nancy had come through to two friends of mine when I was not in the church. I met the medium who passed on the message, a week later, and asked her if she could remember the message. She said, "It was amazing, it was so clear. Nancy said she had come to see the flowers from her funeral, and that she felt like being twenty-two again - she was making strokes as if she was playing tennis" The medium, Anne, said, "I've never seen anyone looking so well, so shortly after passing. Her cheeks were pink her lips were red, her hair was a lovely auburn and she was wearing a beautiful blue dress.".

There followed a number of messages through various mediums, which I will skip.

On the 12th June, I had arranged a sitting with Josie Vale-Taylor, a medium from London, who was visiting the church. She said,

"NANCY IS VERY PLEASED THAT MANY OF YOUR FRIENDS ARE AROUND YOU. SHE SAYS, " WHATEVER WILL MAKE YOU HAPPY, I SHALL BE HAPPY ALSO."

Josie then said, "Later on, Michael, I'm going to say it, I feel you could remarry. In fact I'm sure you will. I'm picking it up but your wife is also telling me, she would be very happy about that, and she does not want you in any way to feel, 'I wonder if Nancy would want me to do that?'"

She is telling you, "DON'T BE IN A HURRY TO DO IT YET! IT WILL TAKE YOU TWELVE TO EIGHTEEN MONTHS TO STABILIZE YOURSELF. WHAT EVER YOU WANT, MY DEAR, IT WOULD MAKE ME HAPPY'. She also says, "YOU ARE MAKING A VERY GOOD JOB OF HOUSEKEEPING". She also says, "THE TREES IN THE GARDEN NEED CUTTING BACK, BUT PLEASE DON'T DO IT YOURSELF, GET A MAN TO DO IT!"'.

I still went to a meditation group each week, under the direction of a medium called Marion, with whom I used to take services at times. She said to me,

"YOU HAD NANCY BEHIND YOU. SHE WAS DRESSED IN A 1930'S STYLE WEDDING DRESS, SIGNIFYING A NEW BEGINNING FOR HER. SHE WAS GIVING YOU ARMFUL'S OF LILAC AND SINGING, 'WE'LL GATHER LILAC IN THE SPRING AGAIN', AND LAUGHING, BECAUSE SHE IS SINGING SLIGHTLY OFF KEY. SHE SAYS THERE IS A LOT OF WORK FOR YOU TO DO!"

Later, she said:

"NANCY IS PLAYING PATIENCE OVER THERE. SHE IS HOLDING UP FOUR QUEENS, AND ASKING YOU TO PICK ONE. NOW SHE IS GIVING YOU A SILVER HORSE SHOE - LIKE THEY HAVE AT WEDDINGS. SHE SAYS, 'GOOD LUCK! GOOD FORTUNE!'"

Just before Christmas, 1990, I received a Christmas card from my 'deceased' wife. Nancy had managed to impress the psychic, Janet Horton, to buy a plain card, write a short poem in it, and post it to me for Christmas. Part of it read,

'ON TOMORROW'S DREAMS, JUST HANG YOUR HEART, MY LOVE WILL GUIDE AT NEW YEAR'S START.'

Whatever its merits as poetry, this cheered me up for several days. In March 1990 I had taken part in a service at the Dawlish Spiritualist Church, in which I had mentioned some of the messages I had received from Nancy. I also read an extract from a book, 'Testimony of Light' by Helen Greaves. A few days later I had a telephone call from a lady called Lily Woodard. She explained that she had been at the service but, having recently lost her husband, she had felt too upset to talk to me. She asked me for the title and publisher of the book I had read from. I gave her the information, but later, thinking it would take her a long time to get hold of a copy, I posted my copy of the book to her. I received a polite acknowledgement.

A week later I had arranged to take my two grandsons and two dogs for a walk on Dartmoor. We explored the old, abandoned, railway line that used to run to Moretonhampstead. After a few hours we returned to the car and I realized that we were near the address of the lady who had asked me about the book. On an impulse, I decided to call and ask her how she liked it. After asking for directions, we came to an ancient granite building with an elaborately carved stone balustrade outside, topped with bright geraniums. The lady, who answered the door with a Jack Russell terrier under her arm, had a lively, intelligent face.

She said she was Lily Woodard, and we were all invited in, to have a splendid, home made tea in this historic house. Lily entertained the children by answering their questions about the carved, wooden curios displayed, and told them of her adventures in the high mountains of the Andes in South America. She said she had particularly enjoyed the book I sent, because she not long lost her husband, Charlie. He had been a leading plastics engineer and a spiritual healer, whose many patients were also grieving his loss.

We were invited to come again, and during the following summer, when on Dartmoor, I called in with children or friends, for them to meet Lily and see the ancient building, which had been part of a monastery originally. It was some time before Lily told me that she too had been receiving messages from her husband after his passing. It was not until much later, that she let me read the notebook where these treasured messages were so carefully recorded.

The friends who met at my house for meditation knew that Nancy had suggested that I marry again, and I had some good-natured teasing about it. I had thought that at the age of 69, I was well and truly 'on the shelf', but to my surprise I had several ladies who now seemed to take a special interest in me. Nancy had held up four Queens. I wondered who the four ladies were that she was thinking of. Giving talks, and taking services, I met many pleasant and interesting ladies, but the only one who really appealed to me was the lady on Dartmoor, perhaps because she was only one who made no obvious overtures to me but remained genuinely friendly. This would be a big decision for two people and I decided to let time pass and get on with a new interest that had come into my life.

The Brotherhood and the Tapes

An old teacher friend of mine, Brian, had had a distressing stroke while lying on a beach abroad. It left him partly paralysed, and after some months, he appealed to me for help, remembering how, years, before I had been healed by spiritual healing. I began taking him regularly to a well-known healer in Okehampton, where the hallway was always full of patients waiting to be seen. The healer, Ted Cornish, talked to me, as he was giving healing to my friend. He told me how, after he was shown healing on a programme on BBC TV, he was so inundated with hundreds of letters and phone calls, not to mention visitors, that he simply had to go away for a time, until the interest subsided, and he could come back to deal with matters in a more manageable way.

One day he asked me to go with him, past the line of patients in the hall, to his lounge. Here he showed me a large wood and glass cabinet, specially constructed to hold a large number of audio tapes. These, he said, were remarkable recordings of famous people who had returned through the medium, John Turner, under an arrangement supervised by The White Brotherhood. He said the spirits who returned had had to undergo the strictest training before they were allowed to tell their story, just as a cast of a play on earth have to rehearse until they are word perfect, but in this case, the wording of the script itself was scrutinized, to make sure it was understandable and expressed clearly, without vagueness or ambiguity. When he mentioned the names of the people who had returned to make the tapes, people such as Pandit Nehru, the first Prime Minister of India, Indira Gandhi, another Prime Minister, King George VI and Florence Nightingale, my mind was full of doubts. Any spirit can claim to be someone famous in order to get attention and the greatest care is needed when this claim is made. However, I thought they might be genuine, and if they were they certainly needed to be brought to the attention of a wider public. I asked if I could borrow four of the tapes, returning them on my next visit.

In the next week, I spent hours, playing and replaying the tapes, until, in the end, I satisfied myself that they seemed to be genuine. They were enlightening, consistent and coherent, and gave me the sense of coming from loving and wise personalities.

The following week I borrowed four more tapes. These were made by, Lord Mountbatten, Lady Mountbatten, Dr Scott and the Reverend Roulston, a Church of England clergyman, grandfather of a member of the group.

I now asked Ted Cornish if I might make copies of all his tapes with the object of publishing them and offering them to a wider audience. He said that he had had several such offers but his guides had always told him to refuse. However, he had already asked them if I would be suitable, and they had said I would be.

I set about copying all the tapes, constructing a catalogue, and advertising them in a new paper, which had recently started, called 'Psychic World'. I decided to do this as a church activity, with all profits going to the church where I was secretary. This saved my having to deal with the Income Tax authorities, as the church accountant would deal with the accounts. I sold £16.000 worth of the tapes, which went to many parts of the world, including Japan, Australia, New Zealand, North America, South Africa, Sweden, Germany, Spain, Portugal and Tenerife, besides the U.K.. Later, it also lead to a lecture tour in Portugal, where I had to speak to mixed audiences, using an interpreter, for the first time, which I found a very relaxing experience, as my interpreter was brilliant, and while she translated the English into Portugese, I could plan the next section of the talk. I was so busy at this time that I rarely had time to listen to the whole of any tape. When I did listen to a talk by King George VI, I was surprised to hear him tell the group that they need not worry about distributing the tapes, as someone would come later, who would do this. I could only conclude that I was to be the one.

As I was sending out these copies of the master tapes, I was hoping that someone who had known these people personally would contact me, to confirm that they were genuine. I found two people who had known the characters in life. One was a gentleman who had for many years been butler to the Mountbatten household. He felt that they were genuine and told me many interesting details about the family. My next witness was a friend of mine, a very well qualified Indian doctor, whose family in India was closely connected with the British Raj. He knew a great deal about Pandit Nehru, the first Indian Prime Minister, and had heard him many times, speaking on the radio in India, and agreed that it sounded exactly like his memories of the man.

I had no idea at this time, that my catalogue would be extended many times, to incorporate more and more unusual and even amazing recordings, linked directly to world events as they were happening.

HEAVENLY MATCHMAKERS
CHAPTER 3

During this time I was very well occupied, as I was copying and sending out tapes, coping with a large correspondence, and catering for myself, and my Labrador dog. In addition my grandson of sixteen years, who lived fairly near, and was being awkward at home, asked if he could come and live with me, so I had to think about him as well. We got on well, as he loved long talks on philosophical subjects, and I let his pop group practice in the house when I was going to be out. However, my personal life was also very full. In the evenings I enjoyed the company of one or two ladies and, of course, the group who met at my house for meditation and discussion.

Nancy's suggestion that I should marry again, was always at the back of my mind, and my old college principal, who lived nearby, thinking I was lonely, kindly introduced me to a very talented lady who was both aristocratic and forceful. She had an interest in psychic matters and was more than delighted when I arranged for her to have a private reading with my old friend George Pratt. Her first love, an RAF pilot, who died in action in WWII, came through at once, gave his name, and said he had been with her in spirit ever since his passing. She had always suspected this, but had never quite liked to believe it.

We got on very well, although she was so forceful, and I think my children, who called occasionally, were surprised to find such an elegant lady sitting on my settee in deep discussion on spiritual and artistic topics. I had a very definite offer from this lady but I felt somehow that this was not to be. I was being drawn more and more strongly to the lady in the old house on Dartmoor. I offered to take her out for a drive, but she always refused on the grounds that I had driven so far to see her that it would tire me. Instead I arranged to go to her church in Dawlish and meet her there for the service. As a little test, we arranged to sit as far apart as we could. Lily had her old seat in the front row and I sat in the centre at the back. Lily had a message from the medium, Dorothy Davies. Charlie said that she must look after herself more and not miss any more meals. Dorothy then came to me and said,

"I MUST COME TO YOU, SIR. THERE'S A LIGHT COMING FROM YOU THAT'S LIGHTING UP THE BACK OF THE CHURCH. (I found this embarrassing). YOU'RE GOING TO HAVE A LOT OF WORK TO DO, SIR. I AM SORRY, BUT YOU ARE! THEY ARE TELLING ME YOU DO WRITING. YOU ARE GOING TO HAVE SOME VERSES GIVEN TO YOU. WHEN YOU SIT QUIET, HAVE PAPER AND PENCIL READY."

After the service we went together to thank Dorothy for the messages. She said, "I thought you two were connected."

A week or two later I sat making notes for an article and was very dissatisfied with what I was writing when some verses came into my mind. The verses were entitled,

WHERE DO WE GO FROM HERE?

The Christian goes to Heaven,
Do the others go to Hell?
Yet the Muslim goes to Paradise,
If he fights the Christian well.

The Buddhist re-incarnates,
The Hindu does as well.
The Marxist ceases to exist,
When he hears the final bell.

They all believe their theories,
About the state called death,
They know where they are going
When they draw their final breath.

They never seem to want to ask,
The ones who really know
Those who have been through that gate,
And come to tell us so.

They tell us that their world is real,
There's perfect justice there,
They work for love of service
And there's work for all to share,

Teaching new arrivals,
Expecting justice firm,
There are no harps in Heaven,
Hell has no fires that burn.

Yes, educating earthlings,
Is a spirit's first concern,
And when each one has learned the truth,
They have to take their turn,

Explaining to the pious,
Their teachings were not sound,
Showing to the scientist,
The truth he never found.

That the earth is just the infant class,
And life's a mighty school,
Of never ending learning,
Where none will end a fool.

For all are going God-ward,
And all will gain the prize,
For the leaders there are noble,
The teachers there are wise.

They hear with sad compassion,
The foolishness and flaws
That earthly leaders propagate
When they lay down their laws

On matters they don't understand,
Because they've shut the doors.

They've shut the doors that lead from earth,
To the finer world above,
The inspiration's turned away,
With the messages of Love:

But truth is slowly seeping
The door the door is now ajar:
One day we'll hush the weeping,
That rises, near and far,

From those who think their loved ones
Have gone, they know not where,
Whose silent tears, express their fears,

That they've gone, they know not where;
But then the two worlds will be one,
In a partnership of love
And Thy Will really Will be done,
Here, as it is above.

One day, Lily was surprised at the message she received from Charlie through a visiting medium. It said,

"THERE IS AN INVITATION. IT HAS BEEN MADE BEFORE AND IT WILL COME AGAIN. PLEASE GO! IT WILL DO YOU GOOD. YOU WOULD LIKE TO BE ABLE TO GET OUT MORE. THIS WILL SOON ALTER".

After this Lily agreed to come out in the car and we made many trips on to the moor. At this point I was allowed to read the book in which her messages from spirit were recorded. In 1990, she had been so depressed after losing Charlie, that a friend had recommended her to go to medium, to whom she was quite unknown. The medium, Dawn, said,

"CHARLIE SAYS, 'I'M ALL RIGHT AND YOU WILL BE ALSO, AMONG A LOT OF PEOPLE'". SHE CONTINUED, "YOU ARE SUFFERING A LOT OF ONGOING STRESS AND IT WILL TAKE A WHILE TO IMPROVE ... THERE IS A PHASE DESTINED ... MATTERS BEYOND YOUR CONTROL... A MOVE OF HOME...YOU WILL HAVE TO THINK CAREFULLY AND MAKE A DECISION IN AUGUST RELATING TO A HAPPENING IN MARCH THE FOLLOWING YEAR...AND THEN THERE WILL BE A STRAIGHT RUN. YOUR TEARS ARE BEING DRIED. THERE WILL BE LESS TEARS ...I SEE A REGISTRY OFFICE. THERE WILL BE A MARRIAGE. LIFE OPENS UP IN AUGUST OF NEXT YEAR.

VERY DEFINITELY ANOTHER MARRIAGE, AND YOU WOULD BE WRONG IN NOT AGREEING. TRAVEL ACROSS WATER. DOES ITALY MEAN ANYTHING TO YOU? ("YES I'VE ALWAYS WANTED TO GO BACK.") YOU WILL, WITHIN FIVE YEARS, AND YOU'LL GET A SENSE OF SECURITY FOR THE FIRST TIME FOR MANY YEARS."

Lily said that at that stage in her bereavement she could not accept that this could be an accurate forecast of her future - it was too much like an ordinary fortune-teller's conventional patter.

There were at least as many messages from Charlie in her book, as I had received from Nancy, but I will only mention a few of them. One said,

"CHARLIE IS BESIDE YOU. YOU HAVE BEEN THROUGH A NOT VERY HAPPY TIME. THERE WILL BE TWO OFFERS FROM

GENTLEMEN, ONE OF WHICH YOU WILL HAVE TO TURN DOWN. HE HAS SEEN YOU SAYING GOODNIGHT TO HIS PHOTOGRAPH.. YOU WILL GET A MESSAGE FROM OVERSEAS".

As Lily could not easily get to her own Spiritualist Church at Dawlish, Charlie came through to a medium in South Africa that he had corresponded with. She recorded his message and sent it by airmail to Lily. It read:

"CHARLIE HERE, MRS. RATSEY, IF I MAY SEND A GREETING TO MY EVER FAITHFUL LIL, IT WAS A TIME OF GREAT SHOCK TO HER WHEN I CAME OVER HERE AT CHRISTMAS 1989. WE HAD SO MANY HAPPY YEARS TOGETHER. TELL HER, PLEASE, HOW OFTEN I AM WITH HER IN THE GARDEN, WHICH WE BOTH CHERISHED. I FEAR IN MY EAGERNESS TO ASSURE HER OF MY NEARNESS TO HER, I HAVE OVERSTEPPED MY TURN. LIL WILL LOVE IT ALL HERE SO MUCH, THE PERFECTION SHE WILL FIND".

On 24th February 1990, Lily had a message at her church. The medium, Dorothy Davies said

"HE WANTS ME TO TELL YOU THAT THE CHANGES THAT ARE COMING UP, YOU ARE TO GO WITH THEM, NOT HOLD BACK. HE SAYS YOU ARE TO GO ALONG WITH THEM! YOU HAVE HIS BLESSING, YOU KNOW THAT! HE SAYS THERE'S TO BE NO MORE GRIEF! I'M HAPPY, I WANT YOU TO BE.
AS THE SUMMER UNFOLDS, SO WILL YOUR HAPPINESS. HE GIVES YOU A BUNCH OF FORGETMENOTS. HE SAYS 'YOU KNOW THEY COME TO YOU WITH ALL MY LOVE AND BLESSING! BUT WILL YOU PLEASE TAKE CARE OF YOURSELF! DON'T MISS ANY MORE MEALS! HE SAYS HE'LL BE WATCHING!"

On 11th May 1991, I proposed marriage to Lily and was accepted. On 22nd May, Nancy sent me a message via Janet Horton. It said,

"YOUR HAPPINESS IS MY HAPPINESS! I LOVE YOU!".
This was followed on 26th May at the Dawlish Church, when Mrs. Davies said to me:

"I HAVE A LADY HERE WHO COMES VERY CLOSE. SHE WISHES YOU EVERY HAPPINESS. SHE SAYS, 'YOUR HAPPINESS IS MY HAPPINESS!'"

The next message from Nancy brought me a welcome sense of destiny fulfilled. It came on 5th June, through Janet Horton. It said,

"MICHAEL, THE MERRY WIDOWER, HAS MADE THE RIGHT CHOICE. HE HAS NOT DEPARTED FROM HIS SCRIPT. THE LADY WILL HELP HIM WITH HIS WORK."

Nancy then showed Janet a map, with two pens drawing parallel lines, showing Michael and Lily going on their way together. Janet said to Nancy,

"Aren't you jealous?" Nancy replied,
"SUCH THINGS CANNOT BE IN SPIRIT! IT'S HARD FOR YOU TO UNDERSTAND WITH YOUR EARTH BRAINS, WHEN WE TRY TO TELL YOU THE TRUTH ABOUT THINGS IN SPIRIT."

This amazed me. I did not know I had a 'script' to follow..

On the 3rd of June, a medium, Anne Lambdon, said , at the Exeter Church:

"I MUST COME TO MR. MICHAEL. I HAVE HIS LADY NANCY HERE. SHE SAYS SHE IS SO HAPPY AND SHE WILL BE THERE. SHE WISHES SHE COULD BE A BRIDESMAID, BUT THAT'S NOT ON.

LOTS OF LOVE!"

On 9th July, through Janet Horton, Nancy said:
"WHEN YOU SAY, I DO, DON'T THINK WITH SADNESS OF THE PAST. THINK WITH JOY OF THE LIFE WE HAD TOGETHER".

She then made a gesture of taking her heart with her hands, and said,

"I WANT TO GIVE THIS TO LILY AND MICHAEL".
Lily's next message came through John, whom we did not know then, but who was later to join the Rescue Circle.

"Charlie says: HE'S VERY HAPPY AND HE'S HAPPY FOR YOU. ALL THE DARK CLOUDS HAVE GONE AWAY NOW!"

On 26th September, I had arranged a sitting with a medium for a friend, Dr X. Neither, Lily or I had ever met the medium, Dorothy Chitty, but we had heard of her reputation and knew one of her clients was a High Court Judge. At the last minute, the doctor was called to take a clinic, and could not attend, so Lily took the booking. The reading, which was very lengthy, showed a remarkable knowledge of her past life and my character and ambitions. It said that, together, we would make a breakthrough against the establishment with regard to spreading the truth about Life after Death, a subject on which I frequently gave talks.

The medium said, referring to Lily, Charlie, Nancy and me,

"DO YOU REALIZE, ALL FOUR OF YOU KNOW ONE ANOTHER? IT'S JUST ALL FOUR OF YOU TOGETHER AND YOU ALL FIT TOGETHER. ALL I CAN SAY IS THERE IS A GREAT DEAL OF WORK TO DO! THE LADY HAS HAD A LOT OF HEALING AND THE MAN WITH THE LAUGHTER ON HIS FACE IS HELPING HER. THEY ARE SITTING IN A GLORIOUS GARDEN WITH ROSES OF

ALL COLOURS, AND THERE IS HAPPINESS. I FEEL THEY ARE MAKING SURE YOU DON'T GET LONELY- BOTH OF YOU! I HAVE NEVER SEEN THIS BEFORE IN ALL THE TIME I HAVE BEEN WORKING WITH SPIRIT. IT'S A LOVELY FEELING AND SHE IS A LOVELY LADY. DO YOU KNOW THERE IS LOVE BETWEEN THE FOUR OF YOU? IT'S AS IF YOU MADE A PACT BEFORE YOU CAME TO THIS EARTH LIFE, THAT THIS WOULD HAPPEN. THEY HAVE GONE ON, AND LET YOU COME TOGETHER... YOU HAVE ALWAYS KNOWN ONE ANOTHER! IT MUST BE WONDERFUL! I FEEL I HAVE FAMILY-NOT FRIENDS! THE LADY IS SAYING, (to Lily) 'THANK YOU! THANK YOU!' I FEEL THEY ARE IN A WONDERFUL PLACE, A GARDEN. IT'S BEAUTIFUL! THEY ARE SITTING THERE HOLDING HANDS. IT WAS MEANT TO BE! IT'S LIKE YOU HAD ONE PART OF YOUR WHOLE TAKEN AWAY: YOU SEEM TO HAVE A TWIN SPIRIT HERE ... IT'S LIKE A COIN THAT'S BEEN BROKEN, BUT IN YOUR CASE, I AM SEEING THE COIN BROKEN, AND THEN BROKEN AGAIN, AND YOU ALL SEEM TO HAVE A QUARTER OF IT...IT'S A GOLD COIN, AND WHEN ITS TURNED OVER, THE OTHER SIDE IS SILVER, SO THERE IS NO DARK SIDE TO IT. YOU WILL BE HAPPY! NO REMORSE, NO LIVING IN THE PAST: YOU LIVE IN THE NOW".

13th October, Dorothy Davies came to Lily at the Dawlish Church and said,

"THIS MORNING, I WAS PEELING THE SPROUTS WHEN HE, CHARLIE, CAME THROUGH. HE SAID, ' TELL LILY, CHRISTMAS THIS YEAR WILL BE A SPECIAL TIME, BETTER THAN FOR A LONG TIME. A SPECIAL HAPPENING WILL TAKE PLACE BETWEEN NOW AND CHRISTMAS!'. HE WILL BE THERE ON THE DAY. ALL WILL BE WELL. GREETINGS TO MICHAEL BEFORE HE LEAVES".

It was on 7th November '91 that Janet Horton said that, while she was washing up, Nancy appeared, and insisted that Janet passed on a message, which said,

"DEAR MICHAEL; FOR YOU BOTH, GOOD LUCK AND LOVE FOR EVER, IN YOUR LIFE TOGETHER. YOU WILL SEE AND DO SO MUCH! WITH ALL MY LOVE, NANCY."

On 14th November, to avoid a large gathering, Lily and I were married in a quiet registry office ceremony at which only two witnesses and the officials were present. The date had been kept, secret, even from family, although some had guessed it was imminent.

On the wedding day, a printed card of congratulation arrived from a psychic friend, Phyllis Hunt. On it were words, in ink; the friend said she had no recollection of having written them. They said,

"MAY THE JOY AND HAPPINESS YOU FEEL TODAY, REMAIN WITH YOU, YOUR WHOLE LIFE THROUGH. THE SPIRIT WORLD REJOICES WITH YOU, AND SAYS, 'GOOD LUCK, GOD BLESS!'. C. AND N."

Charlie's next message came via airmail from Iris Ratsey in South Africa. It said:

"CHARLIE! CHARLIE HERE. NO NEED FOR MANY WORDS, BUT PLEASED TO SAY TO THOSE I HOLD MOST DEAR, MY LIL AND MICHAEL, WE ARE DELIGHTED TO SEE THE FULFILMENT OF OUR DEAREST WISH. WE LOVE TO GUARD THEM AND SAFEGUARD THEIR WORK FOR THE MASTER, CHARLIE".

Within the 'five years', mentioned by the medium, Dawn, we had visited Italy three times.

THE RESCUES BEGIN   PART II
CHAPTER 4

At this time I was asked if I would join a group of meditators, known as the, 'Peace Circle,' which was to meet at another house. There would be a Bible and a Koran on the table and the meditation would be on peace in the Middle East. At that time the situation there was very tense. In the previous August, the armies of Sadam Hussein had invaded and conquered Kuwait. In the November, The United Nations had authorized the use of force to free Kuwait from occupation by the Iraqi armies, and a U.S. lead coalition of some 700,000 troops was assembling in Saudi Arabia, preparing to attack Sadam's forces. Many of the Iraqi soldiers were veterans of the ten-year-long war with Iran, and so we felt there could be many casualties among the coalition troops.

Those who Die in Battle?

'Operation Desert Storm,' to free Kuwait, was launched on 16/17th January 1991. A little later on, when we were in meditation in the Peace Circle, Katherine, our hostess, spoke. She said that her guide, Lee Ping, had asked her if we were willing to do rescue work to help the troops dying in the conflict. After a short discussion we agreed, and immediately, Katherine said she had the captain and crew of a USAAF plane with her. They said they knew they were dead because they had seen their bodies in the plane - what were they to do now? We had no experience of rescue work but we had read a book by Air Marshal Hugh Dowding, the Commander-in-Chief of Fighter Command, during the Battle of Britain. He described many reports by men who had died in action, and were confused as to what had happened to them, but were delighted by what they found when they were guided to their destined place in the spirit world.

This gave Katherine the confidence to tell them that a new life opens up for them now. What they must do is, look for the light and ask for help. Helpers would come, and they could go forward with them to their new life.

Katherine, who was seeing all this clairvoyantly, described how helpers did, indeed, come and the young Americans went off with them. We had done our first rescue! Katherine said that the young men did not appear to be upset by the shock of finding that they had passed out of their bodies. They were cheerful and polite, saying things like, "Gee, Ma'am, we like your lounge. Thanks for your help".

More Servicemen are Helped.

A change in the method of working now occurred. Up till then our two mediums had worked clairvoyantly, describing to us what happened. Now they began to work in trance. This meant that they allowed the spirits to take over their bodies and actually speak directly to us, using the mediums' vocal chords and speaking aloud.

OTHER RESCUES

We felt that helping servicemen who had passed in battle was the purpose of the Peace Circle, but during these early days we had, as well, various other people brought to us to be helped, and we realized, later, that the guides must have had further work in view, for the circle is still working, and doing rescues, fifteen years later. With each rescue reported, there is a case number, followed by an (R) number in brackets, which gives the number in the Rescue Recordings Catalogue – these are not in sequence, as they are chosen to illustrate a theme.

Case 1 (R1)Juanita

One case, was a young girl who had died in a convent in South America. She said, speaking through Katherine,
"What are you all doing? Where am I?"
Group: "You are with friends who want to help you. "Tell us your troubles".
Girl: "I don't really know".
Group: "What is your name?"
Girl: "Juanita".
Group: "Juanita - that's a lovely name, how old are you?"
Juanita: "I was at the convent, I fell ill. They said it was cholera. I went to sleep and I don't remember any more. Where am I?"
Group: "You are in a house in England. We help anyone who is lost to find their way - we are your friends".
Juanita: "The nuns said I had to believe in Jesus - is that right?"
Group: "It is right to believe in Jesus. He was the most marvelous teacher and we must follow him, but for the moment you must look round for someone who can help you. There are friends, or people you have known, who are trying to contact you, and take you to a lovely land, if you will look for the light".
Juanita: "Why can't I go back to the convent - back to school? I want to go back to school. Where are the nuns?"
Group: "We have to explain to you, that you have made the great transition, called death. So many people have passed with the cholera, and now you all go on to a new world, which is much nicer than the old one. You just have

to look for the light and find the guide who can take you to your new world".
Juanita: "What is a guide? I don't understand".
Group: "Do you know a guardian angel?"
Juanita: "Yes! The nuns said I have a guardian angel. Do I have a guardian angel?"
Group: "Yes, you have, and they will show you the way to go - can you see one?"
Juanita: "I see a lady, they call her St. Theresa of the Roses."
Group: "Then go with her. Take her hand and go with her. Can you see the light, as well?"
Juanita: "There is a light around the lady".
Group: "Go to the lady and she will take you on".
Juanita: "I wish I could go back to the school".
Group: "You will meet other children where you are going. You will be able to play with them".
Juanita: "Oh! There's Sister Jo! Sister Jo, what are you doing here? Sister Jo says I have to go with her. Good bye, everybody!"
Group: "Some of your friends will be there already. Good bye"

Case 2 (R2) Four Teenagers

Another unexpected visitation happened when four young spirit people wandered into the circle as our preliminary music was playing. One of them said:

"We saw your light and heard your music, so we came in. We don't know what happened. We heard a screech of brakes and found ourselves walking along the road. What are you all doing? Is this a church?"
Group: "We are sitting here, friends, to assist anyone who is lost, particularly, if they have made the transition and not made their way to the light".
Spirit "This is a church!"
Group: "No, you are not in a church, just a home".
Katherine:"One of them is very anti-church - anti-religion. (To the spirits) It's a natural thing - an extension of this life - nothing to fear - you have a life now to live and that will be wonderful".
Lee Ping, Katherine's guide, now spoke through her, saying to me:
"I bring you greetings from a friend of yours."
Michael:"Thank you".
Lee Ping:"The Tibetan, you call him. I give you his greetings".
Michael:"Thank you, I thought he was here".
Lee Ping:"He is a wonderful soul, way beyond anything I can bring you. He is very pleased to see you in this circle. He says this is a working circle.

This is very important. You have been in many circles to develop yourself, but this one is to give out, and he hopes you can continue. Did he bring you words about service?"

Michael:"I can't remember" (I had forgotten his words, 'for you will be needed', eleven years before)

Lee Ping: "He is pleased. For those who do not know, The Tibetan is a very great master. He is beyond even our ideas - he is a very great, beautiful energy. I would like to tell you a little about the work, for you have been, shall we say, in training. We have brought you some people so that you can understand the feelings of those people. In fact, as I am talking to you, two of the people from the car accident are sitting here, listening to my words. Two of them are here, and two of them have gone on. I will leave you now".

The last two spirits finally left with their helpers. When I returned home, I told my grandson what had happened, as he was always interested. He said he knew the four young people who died in the car crash. They were all fellow students of his at Exeter College where he was studying for his 'A' level exams. He said three boys and a girl died in the accident and he knew the one who hated churches quite well, as they had worked together, painting a mural, in the Art Department.

Telling The Parents

People receive the news that a loved one has communicated in very different ways, depending on their beliefs. Some believe that, 'When you're dead, you're dead!' Others, that when you die, you sleep in the grave until the last trump, and the final judgement. Others receive the news with delight.

I wrote to the parents of two of the boys who lived locally, explaining what had happened. One family never answered my letter. The mother was a teacher at a local secondary school. A member of our circle was a science teacher at the same school, and he promised to keep an eye on her, in case she ever wanted to talk about it, but she never did.

Another mother, Jacki Humphries, was delighted with the news and said it had changed her life. She spoke eloquently on Radio Devon, saying that Spiritualism had saved her sanity, and that she intended to go on a course to try to train as a clairvoyant. She visited the Exeter Spiritualist Church and I heard her son, Philip, pass happy, cheerful messages to her there.

Jacki founded the, 'Philip Humphries Trust', in his memory, to raise money for children's charities, having raised £450 for Comic Relief at his funeral. As I write, fourteen years later, I see that there is an article about her in the local paper. She is holding a Clairvoyant Evening to raise money for a mass parachute jump to raise further money for a local school for disabled children. She intends to take part in the jump, herself. She is now the Resident Psychic on Gemini Radio, and recently, when the expected medium could not turn up, and she was in the congregation, she took the service at the Exeter Church.

As the Peace Circle gathered one afternoon, for we always worked in full daylight, Katherine told us that one of a group of nine soldiers we had helped had just been back to her. He thanked her again for the help he had had, and showed her the area where he was now. It was a land of mountains, which he had always loved, and always wished to live in.

We had now helped a total of about thirty Americans, English, Scots and Iraqis. The war was won overwhelmingly by air power, something against which the Iraqis had no effective defence. As a result, coalition casualties were low, at about three hundred, while the Iraqis lost some 20,000 men.

The War Ends

We had helped a Kuwaiti, when he passed. He now returned through Katherine to say,
"I am so happy now, although I have died. My country is free: Kuwait is free! The flag flies again. Thank you for your help."
This was on 27th February: the official ending of the war was at 4 a.m. on 28th February.

What were we to do now? It was soon explained to us that we were still wanted, as there were many who needed help. It was not that most people had any trouble in passing over to the next dimension. Most were, indeed, met by friends or relatives, as Spiritualists have always said. But with more than eleven thousand people dying and passing out of their bodies each week in England and Wales, if only five per cent need help, then there are over five hundred a week who are temporarily lost and for some of these, the helpers on the spirit side, need earthly rescue groups to cooperate in the rescue effort. It was explained to us that our guides would never bring anyone to us that we could not cope, with and they would be standing guard over us, if difficulties arose. Later when some of us went out, as part of a team, to strange, haunted sites, we were very glad of this.

At this point I would like to pay tribute to Katherine, who founded the Peace Circle, hosted it, and taught us the basic techniques of dealing with a variety of spirit personalities. With some, she taught us to be firm, telling them to respect the body of the medium that they were being allowed to use, and not to wave their arms about for fear of injuring the medium or anybody else.

With others, the utmost sympathy and solicitude was required to get them to trust our advice, and so help themselves. It was amazing to the rest of us to see Katherine and Sheila allowing such different personalities to take them over, so that they could be helped.

Those Who Watch the Rescues.
Lee Ping's Advice

L.P: "I want to take this opportunity to say something about the rescues you try to do. I say try, because I don't think, of late, you have been doing as much as you could. There is much potential in this group to help. You have probably noticed that Rescue is becoming more known about, and this means, in the Spirit World, there are more people pressing to have a chance to move forward. Those who do not manage to come through, begin to know about it, and then they press to be one of the chosen few. Many people who are watching will be of a similar disposition to the one who is talking through the medium, and they will be helped by watching, because you know yourselves, if somebody says something to which you can relate in your own life, you say, 'Oh, that's a good idea, I could use it in my own life', or 'I hadn't thought about that one, myself, perhaps that could be for me.' This is a normal human thing, and it is the same in the Spirit World. They will say, 'But I have been lost like that', or, 'I feel like that', and we bring those that we know will relate to what the spirit is saying through the medium, and, hopefully, it will awaken their ideas as well.

There may be hundreds, if not thousands watching. Do not be worried by this. They are not as an audience is. They are mostly people who are thinking only of self, which is why they are in the predicament that they are in, they have only thought of self prior to coming over. Do not worry that they are all gawping at you.

Now you have many people who can do rescues of all kinds, some of one, some of another. You will find that the ones who come are those who in some way, relate to the way you feel about things, in the sense that you have empathy for their particular problems.

You have to train yourselves to deal with difficult ones, although we have not brought you too many that are difficult. The rest of you must train yourselves to speak up when the spirits come through. You must use all your knowledge, empathy and kindness with those coming through. Each spirit is individual, and you must find what will make them think. So if, say, a religious idea will help one, it will horrify another, and drive them off. So try and find what sort of a soul is speaking to you and find words that will help them.

Lee Ping now said that we would have to be firm with the next person brought to us.

Case 3 (R4) A South African Rescue

This lady, who came through Katherine in trance, was weeping and hysterical. Apparently a band of coloured revolutionaries had burst into a white Protestant Church during a service in South Africa and started to shoot the congregation. She had been killed but did not realize it, and the scene of the slaughter was repeating itself over and over again in front of her eyes. She said, in a clipped South African accent,

"My children, my husband! The Kaffirs have come in with guns - in a church. How could they come into a church and kill people where we pray to GOD?"

When Judy tried to explain to her hat she was dead, she said,

"I can't be dead. What are you talking about you silly woman? When you are dead, you lie in your grave until the last trump. I'm not dead!"

Thinking to change tack, I said to her,

"Jesus said to the penitent thief on the cross, 'I say unto you, today, you shall be with me in Paradise'. That is where you can go now!"

She answered, "You talk of Jesus? I am Christian! I never treated the blacks badly. Why do they do this?"

It took us some ten minutes to calm her and get her to accept the spirit helper who she had previously rejected. He had been waiting patiently for her to come with him into the light.

During all this, Katherine had been experiencing all the emotions of this distressed lady and the tears poured down her face, until the spirit, herself, asked for a handkerchief to wipe her eyes with, saying,

"I feel so silly".

This is the sacrifice that trance mediums have to go through many times in order to help the sufferer to accept and understand the new world that can open for them when they open their spirit eyes.

(It was reported in the Daily Mail, that on 25th July, 1993, ten people died, and forty-one were wounded, when gunmen burst into a South African Church, sprayed the congregation with gunfire, and tossed in a hand grenade.)

OTHER TYPES OF RESCUE

Rescue on earth is the subject of many adventure stories and films. We all fear that our loved ones could be in danger and need rescuing. Just as on earth, rescue can vary from simply giving a child a lost bus fare, in order to get home, up to rescuing stranded passengers from a burning and sinking ship, so, rescue in the spirit world can vary from simply assisting a spirit to wake up, up to saving them from the most horrifying situation one can imagine

Here is an example of the simplest kind of rescue, hardly rescue at all.

Case 4 (R15) Mark the Skier

As various members of the group speak to the spirit, Mark, the word 'group', will be used to cover them all. Mark has a very upper class accent)

Mark: "I seem to be waking from a very deep sleep"

Group: "Welcome! Can we help you?"

Mark: "I believe my name was Mark...it's just that...do you know, I think I have passed over!"

Group: "Yes, my friend, you have".

Mark: "I've been asleep. It's as though I have trouble in focussing my mind, you understand - this is a little difficult. Do you know I never believed there was such a thing as life after death, really, I used to say, 'Nonsense, my friends, you will never wake and find there is life, you will just disappear, and do you know, that is what I seemed to do, I sort of slept and disappeared, so to speak.

I believe I became conscious on one or two occasions, the memory is coming back now, that they did tell me what had happened, but that it was as well to let me rest for a little longer, so that I could regain some energies, you know, because if you don't believe in anything, you know!

It's very strange, really, I understand I'm using a body of a lady at the moment, it has very soft hands, I never had soft hands. Do you think she minds?"

Group: "No, she's glad to allow it."

Mark; "Oh, it's very kind of her. Would you pass on my thanks. It's most kind of her. I'm really coming back now. It's so good to have a conversation."

Group: "Do you see anything anywhere? Look around and tell us what you see".

Mark: "Well I used to love skiing, so I tend to see a lot of snow".

Group: "What do you see now?"

Mark: "Oh, I can see snow, yes I can see lots of mountains, you know, and we used to ski an awful lot, in fact I believe that's how I passed over. Yes, because if you fall asleep in the snow, you know, when you fall, you fall, and we used to say, 'When you go, you go! There's no point in worrying about it at all'".

Group: "Can you see anybody?"

Mark: "Yes! Yes! Oh! I can see people, they're actually skiing! I didn't believe you could ski after death. I mean to say, what! Oh my! I'd have come sooner if I'd thought about it. I wouldn't have left it so long. They told me I was getting on a bit for skiing, you know, that I ought to take it a bit

easier. I never listened to anybody else, you know. No, well, the same as other people".
Group: "Would you like to listen to us now, because we can get you to see if there is someone coming towards you."
Mark: "Oh, you mean someone special?"
Group: "Yes, a relative or some friends".
Mark: "Oh, good heavens! Mind you, I'm not sure if any of my friends would want to see me again".
Group: "See if there is anyone-you may not know them."
Mark: "I suppose ones parents might be here, ones parents, I'm not sure."
Group: "They loved you !"
Mark: "Well mother did. I'm not sure about father. I think he put up with us more than anything, but mother was always there for us. A very nice lady. Oh! Mother is here! Oh, my goodness me! She looks a little younger than when I last remember her."
Group: "She's delighted to see you?"
Mark: "Oh, definitely. Oh, my goodness me!"
Group: "What does she say?
Mark: "Well, she hasn't really said anything yet, she's coming - she's all in violet She is wearing a most beautiful dress. Oh, I think I shall have to go - do excuse me, I shall have to go with my mother... it's very kind of you... yes, I think she will be able to tell me, won't she, why and what has happened and where to go. You will excuse me...I don't wish to seem frightfully rude and everything but - she said to remember my manners!"
Group: "Come and see us another time and let us know how you get on."
Mark: " Yes, very kind, yes most kind."
Group: " Enjoy yourself!"
Mark: " Oh yes, I will! I will! You are so kind. Thank you very much. Bye-bye".

How Do They Do that?

We have often wondered how the guides and helpers bring someone to us who feels that he or she is lost in a dark void.
A lady helper called Mabel, who looked after Mark, explained how she worked. She said, "I have to have a very steady mind. I've always had a very steady mind so they thought I could do this work pretty good." She explained that when they see someone is ready to wake or move on, they put a cocoon of thought around them, a bit like a telephone box, and then they move it right over the medium so that they can slip in. She also said, "I look after some of the sleepers, and when they really wake up we have a celebration and give them a party - we have a real good time."

I think we tend to forget sometimes that there is a working circle on the other side who give their power and knowledge to this work. One lady who had been a research journalist on earth told us that as many as eight helpers may be needed to bridge the gap when the medium and spirit are on very different vibrations. One teacher (Raynor Johnson- see Case 13) describes how he sits in the centre of a small amphitheatre, with helpers around him, to give power and any advice needed to answer questions that are outside his own area of knowledge.

SOME DIFFICULT RESCUES
CHAPTER 5

CASE 4A (R 97) AN AWKWARD CUSTOMER

Group: "Can we help you, friend?"
(He grunts)
Group: "Can you hear us?"
Spirit: "Yes"
Group: "Are you happy?"
Spirit: "No!"
Group: "Then perhaps we can do something about it. What's the problem? I expect you know that – (he interrupts)."
Spirit: "I'm dead! Yeah! If I'm dead, how the hell am I speaking to you?"
Group: "It's quite simple. When the body dies, the soul goes on. The gentleman here allows you to speak to us, so you're speaking through the body of a man."
Spirit: "Then I'm dead!"
Group: "Well your body's dead, but you're alive."
Spirit: "What do you mean, my body's dead?"
Group: "Well the body dies, but you are a spirit, and you go on. The spirit doesn't die, it goes on to another world, and now you're in that world, and we want to get you on to a better place. Can you think of anybody that's passed over, that you would like to see again? They could come and help you!"
Spirit: "Well if I could see them, how can I see you?"
Group: "You'll open your spirit eyes soon. They can see us but we may appear ghostly to them. Now is there anybody you'd like to see?"
Spirit: "Yeah, well, whether they'd like to see me, I dunno."
Group: "Let's have try. Tell us who it is that's going to help you."
Spirit: "Me old gran. That's a difficult one, 'cause she's been dead for donkey's years."
Group: "That makes no difference. She'll be used to it and able to tell you all about it. Now you've got to make a wish, a strong wish to see your gran. We're going to do the same."
Spirit: "Her name was Mary."
Group: "We're going to wish to see Mary. Think of her. Remember her!"
Spirit: "I tell you what I can see – a cow. Well that's not me gran."
Group: "Now you're beginning to see. Did your gran keep cows?"
Spirit: "I dunno! There might have been cows about somewhere."
Group: "Don't think about the cows, think about your gran. Ask her to come to you. You may hear her voice."

Spirit: "Oh, she's calling. I can definitely hear her."
Group: "That's good. What is she saying?"
Spirit: "She's not saying anything at the moment. It sounds like a foghorn."
Group: "Gran, please come!"
(Spirit shakes medium's head)
Group: "No, don't shake your head."
Spirit: "It's my head."
Group: "You're being negative. Be positive. If you can see a cow, can you see a field?"
Spirit: "No, I just saw the cow."
Group: "Is it still there?"
Spirit: "Yes. Black and white."
Group: "Does it take any notice of you?"
Spirit: "No."
Group: "Look round. Can you see anything or anybody?"
Spirit: "No."
Group: "Was there a farm nearby?"
Spirit: "Yeah, there was a farm near."
Group: "What can you see now? Grass?"
Spirit: "No."
Group: "Do you really want to see your gran?"
Spirit: "Yes."
Group: "Then do something about it! Wish! She can hear your thoughts. It's like a telephone really."
Spirit: (Complaining)"It's more complicated than ever. "
Group: "Just trust us. Try and get your gran. to come! Mary, please come!"
Spirit: "Huh! I can hear her."
Group: "Can you?"
Spirit: "Yeah. I can hear her loud voice. I hope she quietens down a bit."
Group: "She'll be pleased to see you."
Spirit: "She's calling me."
Group: "Is she getting closer?"
Spirit: "Oh yeah. She's getting closer all right. As she gets closer, I'm moving the other way."
Group: "No, you're not, because you wanted her to come. She'll take you to a lovely place. You don't want to stay where you are, looking at a cow, do you? What is she saying to you?"
Spirit: "She's calling me name – Timothy."
Group: "Answer her! You'll probably find she's got a nice cottage you can go to. Did you get on all right with her?"

Timothy:"Yeah, once I did."
Group: "Is she pleased to see you?"
Timothy:"You can never tell with her."
Group: "Can you see her?"
Timothy:"Oh yeah. I can see her all right. You don't know if she's pleased or not. She always looks the same. When you start talking to her you'll know."
Group: "Well, she wouldn't have come if she didn't want to. She could have ignored you. She's come to help you."
Timothy:"Oh dear! She's telling me not to be so stupid. Just like her."
Group: "Ask if you can go with her."
Timothy:"She wants me to."
Group: "Go with her. She can tell you all about this new world. You don't have to stay with her if you don't want to. You can lead your own life after she has told you all about it."
Timothy: "I better make up me mind and go with her, I suppose."
Group: "I think you'd better had. This is a step in the right direction. You'll be amazed at what you find. Then you can come back and tell us what you find. Then we'll learn more, you see, and can help other people who get lost, as you have done."
Timothy:"I told you my name, didn't I?"
Group: "Yes, Timothy."
Timothy:"Do you know Middlesex?"
Group: "Yes."
Timothy:"That's where I come from, it's a little village."
Group: "What's it called?"
Timothy:"Oh, I can't remember that, Middlesex is all I know."
Group: "Did your gran. live there as well?"
Timothy:"Yes."
Group: "Then you'll have plenty to talk about."
Timothy:"Oh well, I better go with her I suppose. She's getting a little impatient and I don't like that."
Group: "Off you go, and keep her sweet."
Timothy:"Keep her sweet? How can you keep a woman sweet?"
Group: "You'll enjoy it."
Timothy:"Enjoy it? Huh! Still, thank you for trying to help me."
Group: "Have a good life."
Timothy:"Isn't it stupid. How can you have a good life when you're dead? Ah well! I'll go and try it. It's like putting on a different pair of socks. You don't know if they'll fit till you've got one on. Cheerio!"
Group: "Goodbye, Good luck.

Isobel Talks

After we had had some trouble in helping Timothy, a spirit spoke through another medium to give us some encouragement. She said,

"My name is Isobel. Thank you for persisting with Timothy. We come to give you support, in the same way that you support those in need. Some of our friends do take a lot of persuading to let go. They are suddenly put in a situation that seems totally unreal to them, because they do not understand that they have died. Maybe they have no conception of what could happen to them. Their body has died underneath them, so to speak, so they suddenly find themselves in a very strange situation, where they feel they should not be. It is fear of the unknown that stops them moving on.

Thank you again for the help that you give them. It makes our job this side a lot easier. I feel you struggle on, not knowing if the work you do is really successful, and I would like you to know that it is much appreciated. There are so many people, similar to your last one, who are clogging up the system. There are many, many who have no conception of a life after death, and they are literally hanging around in your world.

This is clogging up the system, and it is not only making your work more difficult, but it is also stopping progress on this side as well, so we need to move these people on, as fast as possible. I just wanted to come and tell you that, and to thank you once again.
Group: "Thank you Isobel".

We now heard a voice with a strong Scottish accent,
M: "Me name is McKintyre"
Group: "Hello there McKintyre"
M: "Trying to move these people on is like rounding up sheep, and just about as difficult.   You get the sheep running around the fields, and you want to get them through the gate. And very often they go in the other direction. Trying to get these beings to move on from the dimension they're in, is very similar. They seem to be very stupid, but we are trying to develop ourselves as well, so we have to develop patience. I was never known for a lot of patience, though you'd think, working the sheep that I would be. But then, I had my wee dog, and my wee dog was very patient, and without my dogs I couldn't have done the job. In fact, I could do with my dogs now, to move on the lads and lassies that will keep sticking around the same dimension.

I keep telling them, 'Look, ye dinna want to stay here, there's a much nicer place to go to. I feel like screaming, and tearing my hair out, and they just take no notice.
(His voice rose almost to a scream as he said this)

They are so stupid, and I say to them, 'Ye should have more brains in your 'heed' by now; ye should have developed a little more intuition. Ye should not be sticking around in this place. There's beautiful mountains and lakes to go to,' and they just want to stay home where the pubs are. I don't know what to do. My frustration is so immense; sometimes, I just want to shake 'em, but my friends keep saying, 'Laddie, ye must not get yourself worked up, because ye canna do the right job if ye get worked up,' but I say, 'I'd be better sticking with me sheep, they're far more spiritually intuitive than these dumb clucks.' I don't know what to do! I think I'd better go off to one of me mountains and sit there and be quiet. They tell me I have to keep persisting, because they're like children, that can't look after themselves, so we keep trying, and that's what we're doing, coming back and coming back."

Group: "Do you have any help? It seems a very hard job."

M: "I chose to do it you see. I was a difficult person, myself; I know I'm complaining, but I decided if someone's difficult, the only way to progress, is to deal with difficult people. So you see, I chose. I have a grumble, but who doesn't? We all choose! You say you have a hard life, but that's what you decided to have – and we still grumble."

Group: "But you have your successes. There are those who go through the gate, so to speak."

M: "Aye! They complain about having their life cut short, and I say 'But you're still alive! What are you grumbling about?' What can you do?"

Group: "Keep on keeping on. You're doing a grand job."

M: "I'll say goodbye."

Group: "Good bye Mr McKintyre."

M: "That's not me real name. I made it up. I thought that'll do nicely."

Group: "You picked the hardest job there is. It's well appreciated."

TRAPPED IN THE DARK REGIONS

During the next seven years, we sat regularly in the Peace Circle, and several other members of the group developed the sensitivity we call mediumship. I was now recording the sessions, which, eventually, gave me a large reference catalogue of the rescues we carried out. There were far too many to be quoted here, but I will transcribe some that illustrate the many different types of rescues we carried out from the recordings I made at the time.

There are many levels in the spirit world, ranging those of unbelievable happiness and beauty, to those lower levels, where those whose earth life was one of selfishness and cruelty find, themselves after death - a world of misery and mutual antagonism. Our next customer, if I may call him that, was one of these. His name was Wilf.

Case 5 (R36)
Wilf: "What you looking at me like that for?"
Group: "Only because we'd like to help you if we can."
Wilf: "I don't want to be looked at like that!"
Group: "Oh, well, we'll look away then. Is there anything we could do to make your life better?"
Wilf: "Fat lot anyone could do to help me!"
Group: "Well, we've helped a few people."
Wilf: "No body seems to care."
Group: "You don't seem very happy."
Wilf: "Would you be happy if you had to live in dark, dirty holes?"
Group: "Can't you go somewhere else?"
Wilf: "There aren't any other places, I've looked. Every corner's got somebody living in it. Sometimes you can't even find a corner!"
Group: "There are lots of nice places you can go to."
Wilf: "I don't think so."
Group: "If you start thinking about nice places, you'll be surprised what happens".
Wilf: "Some bloke was talking to me about nice places, but he can't show it to me. I can't see 'em."
Group: "Well, we might be able to show you something, if you could just listen to us for a bit."
Wilf: (Sarcastically) "Who are we?"
Group: "We are a group, known as a Peace Circle, and we're still on earth, we haven't died yet - and we help, people who have died and who haven't got on to the nice places - they're still stuck - and you're able to use the body of a woman who is a medium."
Wilf: (Interjects – aghast!) "A woman!!"
Group: "So that you can speak to us. She allows you to do this, because she hopes it will help you. Now, as you look about, can you see anywhere in the darkness where it looks a bit lighter - just a little bit lighter? Have a look about!"
Wilf: "No, no houses, it's like ruins."
Group: "Not even a light gray colour?"
Wilf: "No. It's red and I haven't been that way because red's Hell."
Group: "There's no such thing as Hell. That's all nonsense that people made up."
Wilf: "Well, I've been worried about that because I didn't lead a very good life."
Group: "Don't worry. There's no such thing as Hell."
Wilf: "Well, I deserve it."

Group: "The worst thing is what you've got now - being in the dark where you are - but the great thing is to work your way up to the nice places."
Wilf: "But I walk around and it's just that - what do you mean, 'up'?"
Group: "Ah, now we come to it. The way to get up is to ask. Now this is very difficult for some people. You have to say, 'Help! I want to be somewhere better - and you have to say it towards the lightest place you can find, and then you'll find that someone will come who can really take you to the lighter places. I tell you that there are parks and gardens and lakes and nice houses, which are all there, but the only way to see them, is by changing your own mind and saying, 'Please help me - I want to improve, I want a better place.'"
Wilf: "That man's here again."
Group: "What's he saying to you?"
Wilf: "He says I'm not likely to see parks yet, but I could go somewhere that's better than this."
Group: "That's a start."
Wilf: "He says I got to go towards where it's red! I'm telling him I'm frightened that that's Hell. The rest of it's all black and the only light is where it's red."
Group: "Well, walk towards it. If you think it looks dangerous you can always stop. I tell you that's where help will come from. Have the courage to walk towards it - there's no danger - that's where help can come from. The other thing that can help you even further is, if you can help anybody else."
Wilf: "I've tried, but I can't get in. They shout at you to go away."
Group: "Have you a friend there?"
Wilf: "You couldn't be friends with these people - you just couldn't."
Group: "Well, we want to get you a friend. Walk towards that red light!"
Wilf: "Is this man part of it?"
Group: "Yes, he will help you!"
Wilf: "He's the only one who ever talks to you. The others, all they ever do is just shout at you. You couldn't try to help them - you just couldn't!"
Group: "Well, maybe you can't help them, but even if you thought you would like to help them, although they won't accept it, that would do you just as much good."
Wilf: "I've thought lately, I'd like to try and go in and talk to them and say, 'Can't we do something?' Find somewhere better? But none of them will listen."
Group: "If you can get yourself, 'up', get yourself better, then perhaps, you can come back and help them. The great thing is, go towards the light and say, I want to go somewhere better. Show me! I want to see somewhere better."

Group: "Ask the man if he will take you". Go with the man!"
Wilf: "He's the only one that walks upright round here. All the rest are bent right over. I'm walking towards the light! I'm walking!"
Group: "That's good! That's good!"
Wilf: "It's like walking through mist! It's going all pink."
Group: "Keep going!"
Wilf : "He says I've got to walk through this hole - like a tunnel - it's very bright."
Group: "You'll soon get used to it". It's like going into bright sunlight after you've been in a shady place - you'll get used to it."
Wilf: "Oh! It's a house! A proper house!"
Group: "Perhaps you could go in there."
Wilf: "He says I can. It's got a table and chairs. It's lovely. Cor! I'm so glad!"
Group: "Good. You could stay there."
Wilf: "He says I can sleep for a while. Then he'll come and see me again."
Group: "Good! We're very pleased! You have a rest now."
Wilf: "My names Wilf. I'm not talking very loud. I'm feeling very weak."
Group: "You have a sleep!"
Wilf: (Very faint) Bye-bye - thank you."

In sharp contrast to the above, is this account of the rescue of a lady who had believed completely in the teachings she had had in her Chapel. It is rather ironic that these firm believers, who most attack Spiritualists, can be the ones most in need of the help that Spiritualists can give them, because of their holding after death, to the inaccurate teachings they have received.

Case 6 (R30)   A Welsh Lady Who has Slept Since Passing.
Through one of the Rescue Circle mediums (spoken with a strong Welsh accent)
Spirit: "I come from the valleys."
Group: "Do you have a Welsh name?"
Spirit: "I was just Jennifer, or Jenny. I lived in a little house with my husband who was a miner. I feel very weak. I feel as if I have been sleeping for a long, long time."
Group: "Do you feel you are awake now?"
Jenny: "I feel I have just woken up."
Group: "What can you see? Can you see nice things?"

Jenny: "Not really. It's very dark."
Group: "We can find you lovely light places, look for the light. "Look around you! What can you see?"
Jenny: "Just the street lights in our village. It doesn't look the same though. It looks very quiet, it used to be very busy."
Group: "You might see someone coming that you know."
Jenny: "I don't understand what has happened, you know."
Group: "Do you know if you were ill, or in an accident?"
Jenny: "I think I was in hospital."
Group: "Is there anybody you would like to meet - some one who has passed?"
Jenny: "I can't meet them. How could I meet them if they had passed over?"
Group: "Yes, you can meet anyone who has passed over."
Jenny: "How could I meet them if they had passed over? Do you mean I have passed over? But I am talking here."
Group: "You have borrowed a lady's body to speak to us."
Jenny: "Good gracious, the Pastor would be very cross about that. Does the lady mind?"
Group: "No, no! She's very happy because she does it as a service, so that you can be taught. We can teach you to go to the beautiful Paradise."
Jenny: Hold on! Hold on, bach! First of all you say I am dead and yet here I am speaking."
Group: "When you die you have another body."
Jenny: "But I have a body now."
Group: "Yes, a spiritual body, and you have borrowed this lady's body so that you can talk to us now."
Jenny: (Sounding aghast) "You mean like one of those mediums?"
Group: "Yes, that's right."
Jenny: "Good gracious! They were anathema to me when I was around! I used to talk out against them and now you say one of them is helping me."
Group: "That's right."
Jenny: "Good gracious!"
Group: "You know what Jesus said when he was on the cross to the penitent thief,'You will be with me in paradise'. You have been asleep and now you can go to Paradise."
Jenny: "But bach, we were taught in the chapel that we would sleep in the grave."
Group: "Yes, that was a mistake."
Jenny: "A mistake! How could it be a mistake? It says in the Bible how we will wait till the resurrection. You mean there isn't a resurrection?"

Group: "This is the resurrection: you have woken up now, and if you will just listen to us, and ask us any questions you like, we can help you go to the most beautiful place."
Jenny: "You mean there is a heaven?"
Group: "Yes, there is a heaven."
Jenny: "I don't know whether I'm good enough to go there, bach."
Group: "Oh yes you are! There are many degrees of heaven. You might not go to the top one but you might go to the middle one." (group laughter).
Jenny: "Hold on, bach. There's my old mother coming down the street!"
Group: "We told you someone would come! Listen to her."
Jenny: "Good Lord! My Mother!"
Group: "Yes. Has she said anything?"
Jenny: "She's not moving her mouth but I can hear her."
Group: "You can read her thoughts."
Jenny: "Can I? What a funny place this is. She says we can go out of the village and up the hill. We always used to go up on the hill outside. She says we've got to walk up there out of this village. I thought I was sleeping in the yard - you know the graveyard."
Group: "You have left all that behind now."
Jenny: "We are walking up the hill. Oh! It is so beautiful! She says it's just like the valleys but much more beautiful."
Group: "That's right. She'll tell you what to do."
Jenny: "I can see a great light over the hills. Oh, you are all very kind, bach. But this is wrong! I've wasted all that time! She says I died in 1955 and this 1996.

Good Lord! What a waste! What a waste of time. I never meant to waste time and here I've been wasting time."
Group: "Never mind. You have plenty of time now. You have eternity in front of you, it's not a waste of time."
Jenny: "My clothes have changed. They've gone a beautiful white. My mother says I held my mind so tight on the idea of the grave that I got trapped there."
Group: "That's why you were brought here, so that we could help you."
Jenny: "Who are you? I mean the group, who are you?"
Group: "We are a group of people, some of us are Spiritualists and we are a Rescue Group; we help lots of people who get stuck and our job is to help and teach them, so that they can go on - meet their families or loved ones and go on to the Paradise - the heavenly places."
Jenny: "Ooh!"

Group   "So may be, later on, you can go on and help some other people."
Jenny: "Oh! I surely will! I've got to go with my mother now and find all about this."
Group: "She'll tell you. You'll meet some others and more of your family."
Jenny: "Oh! That's wonderful. Oh! : I can hear the choir singing; it's beautiful. I'm going to go with my mother now. Thank you very much because when I was on earth I used to speak out against the Spiritualists. I thought they were dreadful. In so sorry! Please forgive me."
Group: "There's nothing to forgive. We are only happy you are on your way."
Jenny: "Good bye, bach."
Group: "Bye, bye. Be happy!"

At the time, when we are doing a rescue, our one concern is to help the trapped spirit to move on to a happier situation. It is only afterwards, when we discuss what has happened, that we try to understand what it was that caused the person to become trapped. Sometimes it seems to be a complete acceptance that death is the end of existence, and therefore they must still be alive on earth, but be in some kind of weird dream. With others, the idea that one will sleep in the grave until the end of the world, (difficult with cremation), leads them to actually rest in their coffin. This is what happened to our next speaker. At first we heard deep sighs from the entranced medium:

Case 7 (R20)   The Girl in her Coffin
Spirit: "They're all gone!"
Group: "You're not alone!"
Spirit: "Alone!"
Group   "No! You're no longer alone! We can help you now. What can you see?"
Spirit   "Nothing!"
Group: "Is it dark?
Spirit: "Grey, grey!"
Group: "Now, we can help you. You have to start to look for somewhere where it's a little bit lighter. See about you. Look for the light. Is there anywhere a bit lighter. That is where help will come from."
Spirit: "I'm in a box!"
Group: "Look for the light! Do you realize you have died? Passed on?"
Spirit: (despairing) "In a box!"
Group: "We'll help you get out of the box. The box is gone!"
Spirit: "Cold in the box."

Group: "Get out of the box. Come out! Push the lid open! Come out of the box!"
Spirit: "Heavy!"
Group: "You can do it" Come out! Push hard. Come on!"
Spirit: (Heavy breathing) (Faintly) "O- U- T."
"Out you come! Think yourself outside now!"
Spirit: "O-u-t."
Group: "Think yourself out side the box. You'll see some light. Are you out yet?"
Spirit: "Lighter."
Group: "GOOD! That's well done. You've made a start. Now you must look where it's lighter. Somebody will come to help you. Look for them ask!"
Spirit: (Stronger now) "Shadows".
Group: "There are people there."
Spirit: "Shadows of people."
Group: "You are seeing people now."
Spirit: (Wondering) "All around."
Group: "Is there somebody special that you would like to meet?"
Spirit: "My father."
Group: "Ask to see him!"
Spirit: "Father!"
Group: "Can you see him?"
Spirit: (Almost smiling) "He's behind me. I can feel him."
Group: "Good. Turn round and look at him."
Spirit: "No!"
Group: "Why not?"
Spirit: "Frightened!"
Group: "There's nothing to be frightened of. Your father wouldn't hurt you, would he?"
Spirit: "No."
Group: "Well, turn round and look at him then. He's longing to see you. Turn round - he will help you!"
Spirit: "He's so tall!"
Group: "Now you can see him."
Spirit: (Wondering) "He's still got his top hat on." (She laughs)
Group: "What does he say?"
Spirit: "He's holding me."
Group: "That's nice."
Spirit: (A few tears) "I cry!"
Group: "You're safe now! You go with him. Take his hand, walk with him."

Spirit: (Half laughs) "He's lifting me. (Tears of relief) Home! I want to go home!") Cries softly)
Group: "He will take you. Don't worry. You'll be safe now!"
Spirit: (More tears of relief)
Group: "Your troubles are over! Is he talking to you?"
Spirit: "Yes."
Group: "Going towards the nice bright light?"
Spirit: "Yes. I feel warmer."
Group: "Now you can enjoy yourself. Be happy!"
 (Deep breaths)
Spirit: "Yes. Thank you. Thank you so much!"
Group: "We're so glad."
Spirit: "I'm told you do this work for many, who, like me, get lost - get stuck. But it was so easy when I knew how. Thank you so much!"
Group: "We wish you happiness."
Spirit: "Thank you! Thank you!"
Group: "Enjoy yourself."
Spirit: "Please don't stop doing what you do! I'm sure there are many like me. Thank you so much."
Group: "Have you had a very bad time?"
Spirit: "Yes, but it's past, past, past!"

This poor girl's idea of what was possible, condemned her to stay in her coffin. When she knew she could free herself, if she made the effort, she was able at last to enjoy the beauty and richness of life in the spirit world, and, as she said, there could be many like her.

Case 8 (R25) Little Billy Does Not Think He Is Dead
One day a new voice was heard, the voice of a young boy who had died some years before, and had been brought to the group to help him understand what had happened to him. This young boy was a good communicator, and returned fourteen times over the next three years, to describe his growing up, his education and his amazing progress in the Spirit World to a stage where he became a knowledgeable helper. All proceedings were tape recorded so that the following extract gives Billy's words and the words of members of the rescue group. At first we heard two audible sniffs, of the kind that one hears from little boys who have never known the use of a handkerchief. Then a lively cockney accent was heard,
Spirit: "Allo!"
Group: "Hello, what's your name?"
Spirit: "Billy."

Group: "How old are you?"
Billy: Me? Oh I'm ten."
Group: "What happened to you then?"
Billy: "Well, this bloke brought me along 'ere, you know, and then this woman was talking to me just now, this one sitting here. She says I'm dead! Ha ha! I mean that's a laugh, 'in'it? I ain't dead. Heh! Well, I don't think I am anyway."
Group: "Have you had an accident or anything?"
Billy: "Well, I was telling her just now, this lady that was here, (he is speaking through her). Well, I can't tell you his name because it's not right, but my friend stole this car. He's a big one, he's bigger than me, and he said 'Jump in the back', so I did. An' we, went off in the car - I didn't think 'e could drive. An' we went whizzin' down the road, you know. An' the bloody Fuz was after us, wasn't it!" So we drove down there an' all of a sudden there was a sort of a bang, and I don't know what happened. I just got out the car. I saw the Fuz coming so I 'opped it. You know you're not going to stay there with the Fuz round, are you?"
Group: "Do you see anybody around you?"
Billy: "I got me friends over 'ere. I've made some friends. I told this lady, I don't know whether she told you or not, I went home to me Mum, and found me Mum crying. Tried to talk to 'er but she was crying so much that I just couldn't talk to 'er. I don't know what it was. I thought, 'Oh blow it! I'm going out!' Whose going to stay round the flats when you can go out, eh?' So I went out. I went out round. I tried to find John again - I couldn't find him. I couldn't find no one. Every time I talked to anyone they just ignored me, I didn't understand it, really. And sometimes when I talked to people they answered me and sometimes they didn't. I spoke to this bloke and he said, did I want to go and see Johnny. I said,
'Well, where is e?' Where Is e?' I've looked all the places. I can't find him, I've looked everywhere, round the back of the garages, down on the rough land, you know. I've been everywhere. I can't find him!'
'Well,' he says, 'He's in the hospital.' I couldn't believe it. He says, 'He's hurt, he's in hospital. Do you want to go and see him? We'll have go on a bus", he says'. So we got on this bus. T'was ever so funny though. We'd hardly got on it before we got off again. Heh! funny sort of bus. Then, we didn't seem to ask no one, we just went in, and there was Johnny, lying In bed. He didn't talk to me. I tried to talk to him but he didn't talk - I don't understand it. Seems funny, don't it?"
Group: "Have you got a Grandmother who died?"
Billy: "No, just me and my Mum. I've been going back there to ftnd

something to eat but every time I ask her for something she wouldn't give me nothing. Don't understand it! I try to go and get it and somehow it seems to go away from me.

I've met some people that have been OK, Some boys that come here with me. There's a couple of them."
Group: "Did they explain that you were dead and you're now in the next world?"
Billy: "No! They didn't say they was dead, they said that they was just the same. We been living down under the arches, you know, that - what they call it? - cardboard city. We live down there."
Group: " Where were your flats where you lived with your Mum?"
Billy: "Peckham."
Group: "Oh, I know Peckham, or at least I used to. Well, we're people who make a little job of talking to people who have died and explaining what to do next."
Billy: "What do you mean, died? Keep on about died! She kept on about died, this woman, just now."
Group: "I think she's quite right, because when you die you just leave your body behind and go on without it."
Billy: "Can I 'ave a drink? 'Aven't had a drink for ages."
Group: "Do you want a drink of water? Only water I'm afraid. What do you normally drink?"
Billy: "Coke, that's what I like, Coke". (The medium drinks some water)
Group: "Have you lost any relatives at all; gone into the Spirit World?"
Billy: "What do you mean, Spirit World?"
Group: "Well, you call it Heaven. Have you lost an uncle or an aunty?"
Billy: "Aunty Joan!"
Group: "Why don't you think about Aunty Joan? Perhaps she'll come and help you."
Billy: "She's dead I'm telling you, I see the people. I keep going round but none of them talk to me. It's not my fault they won't talk to me."
Group: "When you die, as you call it, you go in to another world. It's still got people in it - just the same."
Billy: "When did I die then?"
Group: "When you crashed - when you crashed with the car. When Johnny got hurt. You got killed. That's why your mummy's crying. She thinks your dead, but you know you're not. She can't see you, you see, when you go back. You can see them but they can't see you."
Billy: "What do you mean? Ghosts?"
Group: "You can call it that but you're still just the same person. You're in a real world and you can meet real people there."

Billy: "What about my mates that I've met. Are they dead too?"
Group: "That's right. They can talk to you."
Billy: "Here 'old on! That geezer's talking! He said he brought me here to try and understand and to listen to you. It's like a bloody school."
Group: "No, not really. You don't have to sit in a classroom any more. You can come here and talk to us."
Billy: "I didn't go to school much (laughs gaily). I was off. Not blooming likely. Cor!"
Group: "Shall we call for Aunty Joan for you?"
Billy: "No! This bloke says 'e'll take me somewhere nice. He's a bit like a school teacher this bloke – but he's nice."
Group: "He'll look after you. Once you find what goes on you'll have a whale of a time."
Billy: "He says we can fly!"
Group: "That's right."
Billy: "Get on!" (Laughs disbelievingly)
Group: "Will you come back and tell us when you've flown?"
Billy: "Hold on. He says I'm to tell you I've been here a very long time. This is not recent."
Group: "Really, can you remember what the date was when you were born.?"
Billy: (Slowly) "1957, I think."
Group: "So when you were ten it was 1967 that's a long time ago."
Billy: "I know. I've been wandering round a very long time. Nobody's understood."
Group: "Well, you can always come here. We love to talk to you and if we can help you we will. If you will look about and ask if some one will help you, usually somebody comes. You've got to ask, and you've got to look for the light."
Billy: "Will they give me somink to eat? I'm hungry!"
Group: "Yes! You can have something to eat. But you've got to ask first. Say, 'Please can you help me?' Then you can have all the birthdays you've missed. But you must look for the light."
Billy: "It's dark down here. That's a funny thing. It's dark all the time, as if the lights are on the lamps. I couldn't understand that, why the day didn't come."
Group: "There is a place you can go, where it's daylight all the time. If you can get them to take you there, you'll enjoy it. You'll see the trees, flowers, fields, animals, birds, dogs."
Billy: "I had a dog once. Skippy, he was."

Group: "You might see him again, too, if you can just get to the light. Ask everybody you see. How do I get to the light?"
Billy: "Well, I'll ask this bloke then, all right? He says I got to go now."
Group: "Good bye."

We will leave Billy here, as we have not space for all of his story. He taught us so much over the next three years that I'll introduce his opinions at points where they help to make matters clearer. As a personality, he was most attractive, lively and truthful as only a child can be. He described vividly the life and teaching in the Children's Sphere of the Spirit World. After going to school and college, he became a useful helper and when the children were killed in a massacre at Dunblane, he was there helping. He returned to us many times and in the end was trained for rescue work himself. The whole story is told in the book, 'Billy Grows Up in Spirit'.

MORE CASES
CHAPTER 6

The next rescue deals with a lady who thought we were mad to think that we could get her dead husband to come to meet her. This is not unusual with people who have dismissed all ideas of an after life as so much nonsense.

Case 9 (R214) Walking, Walking, Walking
Spirit: "I'm walking along this road for ages – and I'm lost!"
Group: "Tell us how you feel!"
Spirit: "I'm tired and I'm lost. I've walked for ever."
Group: "I think we can help you if you wouldn't mind listening to us. Have you been walking a long time?"
Spirit: "Are you kidding?"
Group: "Something has happened to you, rather unexpected. Have you had an accident of any kind?"
Spirit: "No! Just the odd aches and pains."
Group: "Were you at home or were you trying to go somewhere?"
Spirit: "Well, I set out, didn't I. I don't know."
Group: "Well, we're a group of people who've helped lots and lots of people who've got lost. It's easy to help you, if you will listen to us. I must explain some thing to you that, perhaps, you don't know – that is that you have passed over, or died, and gone in to the spirit world. You're just entering it now, and we can help you to go to a lovely place with people that you like. Is it great shock to you to think that you've passed?"
Spirit: "I hear what you say, but I think you're balmy!"
Group: "That's perfectly natural for you to think that. We're often told that we're, balmy but it turns out that we're right. Now, there's one way that you can test it. We'll give you some evidence!"
Spirit: "What's that?"
Group: "Is there anybody that you know, that has already died, that you were fond of, that you would like to come and talk to you, and help you to find out where to go? Who would you like to see?"
Spirit: "I'd like to see me Old Man! And that would be a miracle!"
Group: "A miracle that we can perform! I know you don't believe us, but wait and see the evidence. If you don't mind - trust us and do what we say, which is this: make a big wish to see your Old Man again. Imagine what he looks like and call for him to come to you. Say, "Help me! I want help". Now, we're a group and we're all going to wish for him to come, as well. You may find, after a little while, it'll get a bit lighter somewhere, and

someone will come to you out of the light. Will you make that wish now?"
Spirit: "All right."
Silence............
Group: "It'll take a little time, it may get lighter."
Spirit: "Come on me lover, Let's be 'aving you!"
Group: "Well. Give him a minute. You keep wishing and tell us if it gets lighter."
Spirit: "It can't be, can it? Well! I don't believe it! He's doing it to spite me! He's black – like a coal man - not very nice! He's just walking out like it! He's been gone twenty years."
Group: "It can be! He's come because he loves you. Feel him! Touch him! It's him all right!"
Spirit: (She laughs) "He's telling me not to poke him."
Group: "He's waited for you twenty years! Are you happy now? Is he glad to be with you?"
Spirit: "Oh! Yes! Yes!" (The medium's face was a mixture of incredulity, joy and tears).
Group: "He'll have a nice house all ready for you."
Spirit: (More tears) "Thank you! Good bye. Thank you!"
Group: "We weren't so balmy!"
Spirit: (She laughs) "No!"

As the medium recovered, she still had tears in her eyes. She said, "That was so lovely. He just held out his arms to her. It was beautiful".
We have often found that the state of mind of the person at death, is what settles the state they find themselves in, in the next dimension. If one can change that state of mind, one can improve their situation quite quickly, no matter how long they have been in distress. This well shown in the next case, where a teenager still felt the pain of her injuries.

Case 10 (R94) A Teenager in Pain
Group: "Welcome friend. Would you like to talk to us?"
Spirit: "My head hurts"
Group: "We'll see if we can help you with that. If you'll listen to what we say, we can help you with your pain."
Spirit: "It feels like it's going to explode."
Group: "Oh dear! Did you have an accident?"
Spirit: "I don't remember."
Group: "Now, if you listen to what we say, we should be able to get your pain to go away. But first of all, do you realize that you have died and passed over?"

Spirit: "No, I think it must have been an accident. I'm still in pain, my head is hurting."
Group: "Yes, now we are going to try to help, but first of all, you have to understand that you have passed into the spirit world, and in the spirit world you have a new spirit body, and the body which had the pain, is gone. You're not in it anymore. You are talking to us through the body of a lady who is allowing you to use her body. You are not a body, but a soul or spirit, and the only reason you have a pain is because of your memory. If you listen to what I say, we can probably get your pain to go. You have to say to yourself, 'I will not have this pain – pain be gone! Leave me! You are not my pain. I do not want you. Go!'
I'm going to count to three, and as I count, you must be saying to yourself, that the pain will go. One! The pain will start to go! Two!! The pain will continue to go. Three!! The pain is beginning to leave. It will continue to go now. You must believe this – and it will happen! The pain was only in your memory."
Spirit: "It's a bit better."
Group: "Good. It's beginning to work. It's up to you. You can get rid of that pain. Say 'pain be gone! You don't belong to me.' You are a free spirit with no pain, no aches, and now we're going to help you meet some lovely people and go." (Spirit interrupts)
Spirit: "I'm lost!"
Group: "Of course you're lost, and we're going to help you. We are a group of people who help people who are lost – that is our job. Now, we've got to get you feeling comfortable first, and then we're going to get you to meet someone who loves you, who will help you. As you look about you, can you see anything at the moment?"
Spirit: "Not now, but I did see a car, it sort of rose up."
Group: "That was the accident you see. You are a spirit now, but you can hear us, that's the great thing."
Spirit: "Yes."
Group: "While you can hear us, we can begin to help you. We want you to think of anybody that you love who has already died. Can you think of anybody you would like to come and see you, and help you?"
Spirit: "Grandmother?"
Group: "Now then, I think we can get your grandmother to come, but you'll have to help us. We are all going to wish for your grandmother to come and help you. Then you watch and see what happens. Now, wish to see your grandmother.
Keep wishing!"
Silence

Group: "You may see a light somewhere."
Spirit: "She's probably there. I've got this feeling that I want to run in a direction."
Group: "Run towards her, go! She wants you to come. You might hear her thoughts in your head."
Spirit: "Oh yes!"
Group: "What is she saying?"
Spirit: "Thoughts of love. Welcome my child."
Group: "She'll look after you."
Spirit: "I feel so much happier now."
Group: "Good! Give her a big hug! Is she happy to see you?"
Spirit: "Yes, yes. She's there, waiting."
Group: "Good. She'll take you to a lovely place. I bet she's got a nice little cottage. Can you see anything yet?"
Spirit: "No, not apart from her."
Group: "You'll gradually begin to open your spirit eyes, and see a beautiful world – it's there."
Spirit: "Right! I can see it now!"
Group: "What can you see?"
Spirit: "Countryside, trees. We're walking through them. Life's going to be much better now. Thank you. I'll go with her."
Group: "That's right, go with her. Has the pain gone?"
Spirit: "Yes. Goodbye."

Resentment.
We find it is so important to die without resentment, or hatred of anyone or anything. Resentment trapped this lady from 1955 to 2001.

Case 11 (R126) Hanged by the Neck
On 23rd of August 2001, at about 3.30 p.m., a lady, speaking to us through the medium, said she had been hanged. What follows is a transcript of the recording I made at the time.
Group: "Welcome friend. Would you like to speak to us?
Spirit: "I know I'm dead because the words, 'You will be hanged by the neck,' are embedded in my mind."
Group: "We understand!"
Spirit: "The last moments of my death keep playing them, and I can't seem to get a way from the thoughts".
Group: "We'll see what we can do to help you".
Spirit: "I know I did not obey the law but I still feel resentment at the injustice".

Group; "Now we are a group of people who—
Spirit: (interrupting) "It doesn't make any difference. It still goes round in my head that if it is wrong to take a life, why was my life taken. It's not justice, it's revenge, and my thoughts are on a wheel of coping with the condemnation and resentment and guilt. I feel guilty, for having destroyed someone's life, but if they're not dead when you kill them, why does one have to be hanged by the neck if it is a wrong thing to do? How can it be wrong if they're not dead?"
Group: "In the same way, you're not dead. So although they've hanged you, you're still not dead. You will live for ever and the great thing is for us to get you to be happy and go to the beautiful places that are waiting for you as soon as you can get rid of the resentment - because that's what's holding you back".
Spirit: "I have no sense of time. It seems like an eternity but they tell me it isn't that long."
Group: "What we are here for is to get you to move towards happiness. You'll have to listen to us or we can't help you. We understand your feelings of resentment, but, in a way, the person you killed could feel the same, and it's best for both of you to give it up because there's a wonderful life waiting for you as soon as you can give it up."
Spirit: "If I could give it up, I would have. I don't know how."
Group: "You've made a start. Now, the first thing is this: is there anybody you know, who has already died, someone you were fond of, that you would like to come and talk to you and help you. – a grandmother perhaps?"

A period of silence followed.

Group: "Well, if we can't have a person, did you ever have an animal that you were fond of?

-Silence-

Group: "So you never loved anyone! Have you ever liked anyone? If you can think of anyone you liked, that will be the start of your progress."
Spirit: "In my childhood I had much abuse. If I started to care for any one there always seemed to be a hidden agenda. There was always something they wanted, so I grew up to be suspicious. With any serious affection there was always something they wanted, so I had to keep my guard up."
Group: "We understand."
Spirit: "I am reasonably intelligent, but I am aware that my emotional development was seriously affected."
Group: "Were you an orphan?"
Spirit: "Not really, but it felt like that."
Group: "Have you tried simply asking for help?"

Spirit: "Who can I ask to help me? Even if some one comes to help, I would be suspicious of them. Is there a way to break this pattern?"
Group: "I see your point. Now we meet regularly to help people. We have no hidden agenda, except for the pleasure of helping people. Now there are very many people like us in the spirit world because the spirit world is enormous, much bigger than the earth, and it's full of millions of people, and some of them are very loving. All they want to do is to help you, and they can help people like you; so if they do come to help you, please trust them. They can't do any harm. They simply want to help you break the pattern – and then you can start to progress. Now, a few questions; are you in the light or the dark?"
Spirit: "My emotions tell me it is dark. My eyes tell me that it is gray."
Group "Do you see any people at all?
-Silence-

The world where you are is full of people but you can't see them because you haven't opened your spirit eyes."
Spirit: "Probably because I don't want to."
Group: "Because you suspect them."
Spirit: "Yes."
Group: "Most of them are only wanting to help you and the ones who don't are probably not on your level anyway. You have got to learn to trust – then you can break the cycle. If I could just tell you this: life in spirit is many times better than life on earth – it is so wonderful, yet you are held in the dark by your own thoughts; so we've got to try to break these thoughts. Now! Without asking anybody in particular, have you ever prayed to God? There is a Divine Being who creates all life. This could be your start. Say, 'Please, God, help me! Help me to break out of this cycle and see the wonderful world that lies ahead of me!' Do you think you could make that effort and see what happens? We'll make the effort with you and then keep quiet while you watch. It may get lighter. Make the big wish, 'Please help me! I don't want to be in this cycle anymore.' Tell us if you see a change! Ask to see the light!"

-Silence-

Group: "Tell us what you see!"
Spirit: "I don't see anything. I feel an expansion. I feel I could sleep now - I feel I can rest at last!"
Group: "That may be the best – this may cure you. You have started to progress. God Bless you!"
Spirit: "Thank you".

As the medium came out of trance she said, "I was given the name Ruth. I felt a simply wonderful feeling of relief at the end".

Case 12 (R19) A Victorian Courtier Awakens

One day, an interesting man, who passed in the days of Queen Victoria, was brought to speak to us. He was a high-minded aristocrat, a courtier of the Queen, who totally believed the teaching of the Church of England of his day, that after death, one would sleep in the grave until the end of the world and the final judgement. His name, Fortescue, is very well known in Devon where members of his family have been wealthy landowners, and to this day have acted as royal representatives in the county. He never gave his Christian name, only his surname, as was the custom in his day. He said he had been very bored waiting, and had patrolled the corridors of Buckingham Palace where he found himself totally ignored by everyone.

He asked who we were, and at first, was completely contemptuous of us as Spiritualists. I asked if he disapproved of Queen Victoria having John Brown as her personal attendant and private medium, keeping her in touch with her beloved husband, Albert. (I knew this because both the Queen and John Brown have returned, and I have recordings of their talks in the catalogue.)

"So she thought," he said, with obvious distaste. I asked if he believed in angels and he said he did, so we asked him to look for the light, and waited. After a while he spoke,

"Oh! How beautiful. An angel!"

We realized that the guides had appeared to him in that form. After we reunited him with his father, he returned several times to report his progress. On his third return visit, he said,

"Good afternoon! I said I'd come back again to tell you what happened to me. Fortescue, speaking! You have a lovely day here today, really lovely. Well, I think I'm coming along. I've been to all sorts of places in the spirit world and I think I shall be doing some work shortly that will help other people who were badly lead to believe the wrong things, and consequently got caught as I did.

I'm having to catch up with the modern things. I'm finding that some things, which were only in embryo in my day, have come and gone (he pronounces it as 'gorn'). It's rather exciting! Most interesting to see what has happened to the Royal Family – they seem to have got themselves into an awful bother at the moment, unfortunately (he speaks in March, 1996) – which is such a shame. You see, there were bothers in our time, but it was not flaunted in public – it wouldn't have done. It's all so different now, and it's quite exciting to find out all these things – some good and some bad, but what was bad in my time has now been relieved in many ways. You still have poverty in some ways, but it is not so bad as young children dying in the street, and being used very ill at work, and such like.

Today you have poverty of a different kind which I would call spiritual poverty – do you not agree".

"Yes, we do".

"This must make it very difficult for you, in the work you're doing, and I really do appreciate it, because you helped me so much, and I intend to help you in return, if I may.

There are many who were caught as I was, and it seems that there are quite a few who are beginning to wake up at this time. I suppose I was one of them, we were held so much by the Church's teaching, thinking that no other thing could be right, and that you slept in the grave – and so we sleep! What a waste of time that is! I get quite cross when I think about it. Of course, I'm not in the higher regions yet, and it's true that I lose my temper, and this does not help me, and so I have an awful lot to learn, but there is so much love and understanding about. Somebody comes immediately when I feel like that and sits and talks to me until I come out of it, and realize it's no good feeling angry about it – it does no good at all, and takes you completely in the wrong direction.

There is a group of people attached to her Majesty, as I was myself, and they have over the years tried to help people such as myself. Apparently I was rather a bad case, you know. I was extremely difficult. It would help a great deal if there were more groups like, this where we could bring people, but I can tell you that, when you were helping me, several others were able to listen at the same time, and they have been helped as well. I was extremely lucky that I was the one able to speak to you, and at the same time, some of what I believe you call Karma, has been lifted, because I did it. Help has come to me, and I do realize that my views of things were not right, but, nevertheless, I have no doubt that there is a God. I am learning to look at that in a totally different way, you might say. When I was alive I would pray to my God for this and that. If something was not right, I would ask him to put it right, not realizing that it was I, myself, who should put it right. My God was, omnipotent – I am trying to find the right words – he was a vengeful God in some ways. We were told to fear God. How stupid! Now, when you come into the light of this world, you can feel the love that is God, and you know there is not a morsel of vengefulness to fear. On the other hand, I know I'm not going to see the face of God that quickly, but I have seen some good souls and I realize I have an awful long way to go.

I think I am going to have to go now – the energy going. It's been awfully nice to talk to you and I do hope I can come again. Thank you again, so much. Good afternoon."

CASE 13 The Scientist Returns.

I would not like my readers to think that our circle only dealt with rescues. Of the well over seven hundred recordings of spirits speaking through our mediums, about a third are rescues. Spirits come to chat, to teach, even on one occasion to flirt outrageously.

It was on 12th November 1992 that a new male voice, with beautiful diction, spoke through Sheila. It seemed that the speaker was a trained and knowledgeable teacher. He said he had known the medium in Australia. When he said 'The watcher on the hill is the higher self,' I suspected who he might be and asked him if he was the author of a book, "The Watcher on the Hills". He replied, 'Yes', and I knew we were listening to Dr Raynor Johnson whose books I admired, and whom Sheila and her family had known in Australia.

Dr Johnson had been the Master of Queen's College in the University of Melbourne for thirty- three years, and, as well as having been a research scientist, he was well known as a writer of admired spiritual books, such as 'The Imprisoned Splendour', 'The Watcher on the Hills,' and many others. Dr Johnson had sat with a famous medium and had written extensively on Life After Death.

When he asked us if we would like him to come again, and give us a talk on 'God Consciousness,' we all agreed. Raynor visited us regularly for a over a year, speaking through Sheila on a succession of different subjects. This gave me the opportunity to ask him many scores of questions on subjects which puzzled me, which apparently earned me the name of 'The Questioner', on the other side. When I asked him if he found anything different from what he expected after death, he replied,

"The only thing unexpected is that it is more wonderful than I thought it could possibly be. To be rid of a body that is beginning to deteriorate, to leave a mind that is becoming confused, simply because the physical deteriorates, to meet up with ones relatives and ones friends that one loved – not the ones you don't love – who are not around on your level; to experience the inner peace which we should all be able to experience on the earth plane, but sadly do not. To go wherever we want to go, to study in the Halls of Learning, to have many more books – I was in my element – eternity would not be long enough - but that would not be heavenly for every one, would it?"

We had never had a failed session, where no one came to speak to us, but one day we waited for many minutes in silence. Then an enormous smile spread over Sheila's face and she took my hand very warmly and said,

"Oh! My dear!" I said,

" Is it Nancy?" she nodded, and I said,

"So, you've managed it! It's a wonderful thing that you've come!" She replied,

"I come not to cause you pain, but to thank you for our life together." I replied, "I thank you every day!"

She continued,

"You have done such good work and we are helping from this side – Charlie as well. He sends love to Lily, of course".

Raynor spoke next to say,

"Our friend Nancy asked if she might come through. She did not want to push in, until we had finished the book. We feel the emotions of the astral when we return and I, too, felt Nancy's emotion, for we have to work together very closely. There is a point where we are all in the one body, the medium, Nancy and myself".

Earlier in the year I had had an article published, explaining that Raynor Johnson had returned. Through the newspaper, I then received a letter from a well-known writer, Paul Beard, saying that Raynor Johnson had been a personal friend, and he had been waiting for his return. He asked if he might listen to some copies of the tape recordings we were making. I knew Paul was a director of a publishing firm, and, also, was the author of several respected books, such as, 'Living On,' and, 'Hidden Man'. He had also been the President of the College of Psychic Studies for nineteen years and was probably the most experienced assessor of mediums in the country.

After he had had several copies of the tapes, he asked if might come down to Devon and sit with the group. He came down from London on 'The Golden Hind' train, and I took him out to lunch, and on to our meeting. Raynor soon came through Sheila, and he was obviously very affected by the meeting with his old friend. It was fascinating, listening to the two old friends chatting to one another, and when it was over, Paul turned to Sheila and said, simply, 'You have achieved'.

As I took Paul to catch his train to London, I gave him a copy of Katherine's book, 'Soul Trek', which she had printed privately, and it was due to Paul's interest and influence that 'Soul Trek', and 'In Touch with Raynor Johnson', were published by Light in 1996, and both our mediums went to the press launch, in London, at The College of Psychic Studies.

Raynor explained that for 33 years, he had been able to teach 1,000 students a year, something of spiritual truth, during his time at Queen's College. He had passed in 1987, so it was five years after his passing that he began to teach us in November 1992. He emphasized the importance of having knowledge of the after life before one dies. He said:

"It is since I have come to this side that I appreciate the teachings that I was given myself. I can only reiterate that I had some very good teachers so that I was able to impart the information to my students. I did have help from a lady who was a medium, and she was able to give me a great deal of information and taught me how to go deeper into meditation, and how important it is, particularly as we gets older, to seek the nature of life after death. There is so much information. You hear people say that nobody has come back to tell us. This is so ignorant and so futile; it leaves people in the dark. You would not go on a journey without gathering information about where you were going, and how you were getting there. So, instead of passing over, totally confused as to what has happened to you, you can go on your journey knowing your destination and not be shocked, having to be treated almost like going to hospital.

Those who pass over are helped, but sometimes they will refuse to be helped. They close themselves off with their minds, so that they do not see us when we want to help them. It is better if you pass over with your eyes and your mind open. There are so many who say, 'I don't want to know'. This is very sad, but we do our best, do we not?"

It was of interest to me to hear that even such a clear and logical thinker and talker as Raynor Johnson became confused at the end of his life, because the 'physical deteriorates', yet he regained full mental clarity after passing. I have known of people who suffered from Alzheimer's, and did not know their relatives, who were able to communicate clear, loving messages to their family after passing, so the confusion, though distressing, is only temporary'.

DO WE ALWAYS SUCCEED?
CHAPTER 7

We are always surprised by the fact that rescue work becomes so easy when there is a group in the afterlife, supervising and arranging most of the work of bringing people in need to us. A spirit may have been in limbo for years of our time yet they can be helped and united with a friend or loved one on the other side in less than ten minutes. As the little girl in the coffin said, "It was so easy when I knew how". Here I bring accounts of rescues that were not entirely satisfactory – at least at first.

Case 14 A Catholic Priest in Distress.
Spirit: "I was a priest, but I lost my faith. There was always a feeling that, even if I doubted, possibly Jesus would save me, or else, that possibly the doubt would prevent the help coming. It left one with a great feeling of confusion.

So you go through the motions, because, as you say, it is a living. What else could I do if I didn't do the work I was trained for? The doubt seeps through, until it comes through the very bones. It's very distressing to have to go through the façade (of believing) and trying to take care of other people's fears. It was my own crisis, which caused me to walk into the sea. I could not cope with any more of this pretending – I did not know what to do!"
Group: "We understand".
Spirit: "Even if you have help from your fellow priests, or your superiors, there is always that stain left in somebody's mind, that you are not to be trusted, because you have this doubt. If you are fortunate in having someone you can go to who, has a broader view of religion, you are indeed fortunate, but, unfortunately, most of your superiors are locked into this aspect, instead of allowing you to develop, using your particular faith as a stepping stone.

The Church is supposed to be a body full of people with different views, but it has come to mean just people who have to follow a particular way of looking at things, which stifles the growth of the spirit".
Group: "Are you not consoled by the knowledge that your doubts were right? It was your search for truth that brought you to the crisis".
Spirit: "That's all right for me, but what about all those others who are still suffering as I did?"
Group: "You must convince yourself that you were right, and rise above all this suffering. Then you may be strong enough to help others".
Spirit: " Perhaps you are right. The crisis has not passed for me yet".

We were not able to help this man further and hoped he would find a way out of his difficulties. We could not classify this as a successful rescue.

CASE 15 Mariella. A Flirtatious Spirit.
Our efforts to lead this lady to a more purposeful way of life were not at all successful, but they amused the rest of the group very much.
Michael: "Hallo friend, would you like to speak to us?"
Spirit: "How did you know I was here?"
Michael: "We guessed."
Spirit: "I was a little curious."
Michael: "There were some slight changes in the medium which indicated to us that there was somebody there."
Spirit: "Oh. I was very interested in you (looking at Michael) you are a very attractive man." (Group laughter)
Michael: "Also a married man."
Spirit: "Your wife's not here, and I usually get on with wives very well."
Michael: "Tell me, could we ask your name? We are very interested."
Spirit: "Mariella. Most men seemed to like my name."
Michael: "I think so. Did you come from this part of the world?"
Mariella: "Oh it doesn't really matter does it? So long as we are together (more laughter) I always found the company of men so much more – stimulating you could say."
Michael: "There is another gentleman here."
Mariella: "Oh, I think I rather like them tall."
Michael: "Yes". (laughter)
Mariella: "And I think you are quite good looking."
Michael: "Is there anything we can do to help you in any way because that's the purpose of our group? "
Mariella: "No."
Michael: "Are you happy in your life?"
Mariella: "Mm, I just sort of drift around, you know."
Group: "Is there anybody else there?"
Mariella: "Oh, I expect so, not with me particularly, no"
Group: "Do you see them?"
Mariella: "Oh, occasionally they send someone to talk to me."
Group: "And do you listen to them?"
Mariella: "Not if they are ladies, no."
Group: "Isn't that a bit unkind if they have come to see you?"
Mariella: "I don't intend to be unkind, my dear, not at all, it just seems to be the way I am. I'm extremely boring."
Michael: "We are very interested in what it is like for you, your life. Is it

pleasant, are you in pleasant surroundings?"
Mariella:"Well most of the time it is, sort of: there is no real purpose so you have appeared in my consciousness and this gives me some focus."
Michael:"Yes."
Mariella:"Though life I seem to drift."
Michael:"Have you been drifting for long?"
Mariella:"I've no idea really. Um, it seems to be quite a long time. I must say I don't get a chance to meet with very nice gentlemen like you these days."
Michael:"It is very nice of you say so. What I am interested in is, do you have a house of your own where you live, or do you just drift?"
Mariella:"Well, I really stay with friends."
Michael:"Do you, yes?"
Mariella:"And then I (flirt) if I can."
Michael:"Do you have any teachers who come to teach?"
Mariella:"I don't seem to be able to concentrate very long. I suppose in a way, some people have said to me 'Now look Mariella, you can't keep drifting through life like this, you must bring your mind into more serious matters.' And I say life is too short."
Group: "Which life is this, Mariella?"
Mariella:"Well, any life really."
Group: "Are you talking about the life on earth when you had your body, or the life in your spiritual body?"
Mariella:"Well both I suppose. Well I intend to take one day at a time. You see when I was here on the earth plane there was always the rather unpleasant things one had to do, you know when one's nails got broken, it was disastrous, one's nails had to be correct, people would say, 'Oh! She's not looking after herself, she must be slipping.' I tried not to think about the dreadful things in life. Um, you know they're there and you know there is such a thing as death, but of course, I never really... I tried not to think about it, do you understand?"
Group: "Were you married?"
Mariella:"Oh several times."
Group: "Did you have any children?"
Mariella:"Oh no!"
Group: "Are any of your husbands with you?"
Mariella:"Well they occasionally pop in and say hello."
Group: "And do they try to talk to you?"
Mariella:"Oh yes. They are always trying to get me to take life more seriously."
Group: "Don't you think that maybe it would be good idea to listen to them?"

Mariella: "Oh, they are always trying to tell me what to do, my dear."
Group: "Wouldn't it be nice not to keep drifting about like this? Wouldn't you like to see something more stable?"
Mariella: "Um. (Paused as if thinking) I don't quite know how to go about it."
Group: "That's why you have been brought here, so that you can begin to think about it- while you are in this body, that you are using . If you try, you will find that you can begin to think more clearly. Maybe what one may call 'see a light', the light at the end of the tunnel. You see, it's up to you to think of something positive, something you would really like to do, to learn, and then you would be given help. You can't expect everyone else to do things for you."
Mariella: (There were several 'uh huhs') during this latter explanation)

"I would love to be truly knowledgeable. I've always felt that somewhere in the background I had a lack in absorbing knowledge. We were brought up to feel that to be feminine, and a lady, was more important. A good education was not for us, so in a way you became steeped in this image of oneself; so any leaning towards book learning, or manual labour, was rather frowned on. You had to be able to direct the servants, and you had to be able to hold charming conversations with interesting men, because one's husband wanted one to be attractive to other men, but slightly out of reach, you understand?"
Michael: "Very well put."
Mariella: "So that they would be admired for their..Um.."
Group: "As an ornament?"
Mariella: "An ornament, yes, rather than for their attainments, rather than for your own (self)."
Group: "Now you can think for yourself, and on your side there are many, many schools of learning, on many levels, and it is much easier to learn than at schools here. Now if you would listen to some of the people who come to you, they would be delighted to take you and show you these places. They are really beautiful places. It's not like our schools, don't think that. They are delightful places. It's very easy to learn and you would have companions of similar interests."
Mariella: "Perhaps they would be able teach me through conversation rather than books, to begin with, do you think?"
Group: "Books are easier there, so there is no need to worry. You will find the teaching methods there far superior to ours and you will have a wonderful time."
Mariella: "The wonderful time appeals to me greatly. It would be very nice to be able to develop one's intelligence, putting one's intelligence to some

good use instead of being an ornament."
Michael: "And to help others. I feel you have the potential to learn and then to teach."
Mariella: "Mm, it's a pity you can't come with me." (More laughter)
Michael: "Unfortunately, I've got to wait a little while at the moment."
Group: "He's got too much to do here."
Mariella: "Yes, I can feel his goodness."
Michael: "If you want to ask any questions of anything that would interest you, we will try to answer them from our knowledge, but where you are you really have the chance to get ahead, because it's so much easier to learn there, once you set your mind to it. That's all that is required."
Mariella: "Ah, that's the problem, isn't it? I believe I have a good mind and I can usually see through situations fairly easily, but because of the habitual things that happened to me, I have taken the habit with me and I think I need to learn to concentrate. I think concentration could be part of the key, and listening, the other."
Group: "Well, ask for concentration and it will be given to you."
Mariella: "Mm, I will try that."
Group: "And ask for places, things, to be shown to you and then your choice…"
Mariella: "Will be (easier), yes. That sounds as if…"
Group: "You could do it."
Mariella: "I could try, I could try."
Michael: "Behind will, is desire. Once you want it, you will have the power of concentration and then comes the help. We wish you success."
Mariella: "I think some of my thoughts must be kept to myself."
Michael: "Perhaps that's as well"
Mariella: "Thank you very much for your help."
Group: "Thank you for coming to us."
Mariella: "I will stay around for a while."
Group: "Come again sometime."
Michael: "Yes, please come again"
Mariella: "Oh, thank you. Good afternoon."
Group: "Good afternoon."

Note: On the way home, Sheila felt that Mariella was still with her, and she said to her 'You were a bit naughty with Michael,' and she replied 'Isn't it delicious?' She also said her surname was Florentine.

Case 16 (R20) Letitia – So Selfish.

Although Rescue Work is one of the things that distinguishes Spiritualism from nearly all other western religions, and it is a great privilege to be able to do it, it does have its lighter side in the amazing characters we meet. One afternoon a lady called Letitia burst into speech through the entranced medium, Sheila. Her voice rang out clearly:

Letitia: "I didn't want to die so soon! I protested strongly against this. I thought I was entitled to live a complete length of life and I was whisked away so soon. This was not of my making, I did not agree to it. I understood you die eventually but certainly not at a young age. I was most indignant about this. I found myself on the other side, mixing with people of such a low, low nature. I was furious.

I intended to live in the type of place that I always expected myself to be in when my time came, and I certainly did not expect to go at such an early time. I spoke to everyone around me and I demanded my rights. No one would listen. I was used to having servants and I was very, very angry. Why did I not have my servants with me? I should have someone to attend to me at all times, you understand, and I demanded this, but no one would listen and here I am, alone, with dreadful people around me all the time, at a distance you understand, at a distance. I would not let them come near me, such people of low mentality. Even now I am very cautious as to whom I speak with."

Group: "It is nice that you will speak to us then."
Letitia: "I have been brought here under protest, Madam. I don't see why I should be here."
Group: "We would like to be able to give you some help."
Letitia: "I don't need your help, Madam."
Group: "Can you tell us how old you were when you passed over?"
Letitia: "I was a mere 50 which is just the twinkling of an eye."
Group: "You see where you are, age does not matter. You can change your life and be happy whatever your age."
Letitia: "What is happy, what is happy? Happy is having my jewellery around me. Happy is living in the kind of house that I choose! I prefer to live in the manner to which I was accustomed, you understand."
Group: "Yes, we understand all right."
Letitia: "It's not fair. I have told everyone over and over again."
Group: "Did you live in a house like that?"
Letitia: "Of course, my dear, of course."
Group. "And did you help other people around you?"
Letitia: "Oh definitely not!"
Group: "Why not?"
Letitia: "They must help themselves."

Group: "Don't you think that was rather selfish of you?"
Letitia: "You dare to tell me that I am selfish?"
Group: "Yes!"
Letitia: "Humph!"
Group: "Were you never aware of the suffering of people around you?"
Letitia: "That was their business, it was nothing to do with me."
Group: "Why was it nothing to do with you?"
Letitia; "I did not put them in this situation."
Group: "But how would you have felt if you were in an unhappy situation and nobody was prepared to help you?"
Letitia: "Nobody cared for me when I demanded it, you understand."
Group: "No! I don't understand and I don't think you understand yourself. Perhaps your situation is because you did not show any compassion to others around you."
Letitia: "It is, may be, because I do not understand what compassion is. No one has shown it to me."
Group: "Have you never cared for anyone in your life?"
Letitia: "Definitely not."
Group: "Did you not have a child or a husband?"
Letitia: "No."
Group: "You were a single lady?"
Letitia: "I was a single lady. I did not think any male good enough."
Group: "Did you have an animal, a dog?"
Letitia "No."
Group: "What of your parents?"
Letitia: "They are dead".
Group: "Did they show you compassion when they were alive?"
Letitia: "No. None whatsoever."
Group: "But if they are dead, so are you. Perhaps they might come and help you if you called them and asked."
Letitia: "I must say I had never thought of that."
Group: "There are people waiting to help you when you want it. You just have to ask. The whole secret is to ask for help."
Letitia: "I am in pain all the time!"
Group: "We are very sorry to hear that."
Letitia: "I did have arthritis rather severely."
Group: "Well that can be completely –"
Letitia: "It made me very irritable."
Group: "That's quite understandable, but you can be completely cured of your pain, and can be brought to a situation where you will feel very happy...but you have to open your heart."

Letitia: "I do not know how to open my heart."
Group: "You have to wish the best for others so that they may be happy, seek to make others happy."
Letitia: "The problem is, dear sir, that when you are enfolded within, there is so much pain, and so much darkness, it is very difficult to think of anything else but the pain. If someone could come along and direct me how to deal with the pain then maybe I would be able to consider other people."
Group: "I think the first thing you have to do is to is to look for the light, wherever you can see a light. Look to the light, and ask for help. In this way all the solutions to your problems can come, and you will find yourself out of the difficulties of darkness and pain. There is indeed a paradise waiting, but you have to look for the light, you have to pray, you have to ask for help."
Letitia: "But who do I pray to? Is there a God that they speak of?"
Group: "There is indeed a divine being beyond our comprehension, who understands everything that you think and feel."
Lettitia: "But will they understand me?"
Group: "Yes they understand everything about you."
Letitia: "Me! Me!"
Group: "Yes, they know everything about you, and if you ask for that help it will be given in a way that will seem like a miracle to you. You will be amazed how quickly you will feel happy, how quickly your pain will go, how you will find yourself in lovely places with, kind compassionate people; but you have to make the first step, seeking the light and asking for help. You have the love of this group to go with you. While you are with us, ask for help now. Don't demand - ask."
Letitia: "It will take a little time."
Group: "When you see someone, listen to what they say and don't reject it out of hand. You see you have a guardian angel, you have had one all your life."
Letitia: "Have I? I've never seen him."
Group: "No! I know you haven't, but you could see him now if you wanted to."
Letitia: "Do you think he could help me with my pain?"
Group: "Of course. Yes. He is waiting there. Waiting for you to ask."
Letitia: "I will consider what you have said. You seem to be a reasonable type of people, and you sound most cultured. I will leave you. I have told them I am going to go now. I insist."
Group: "We send you out love."
Letitia: "I will consider your words. You have spoken most kindly to me. You are the first to speak so kindly to me for some time, and if I have a

guardian angel as you say, I will speak to him in my mind and maybe he will help me with my pain. I give you 'Good Afternoon'. "
Group: "Try to remember to say 'please'!"
Letitia: "This is very difficult. I will consider the matter."
Group: "Please!"
Letitia: "Thank you. Goodbye."

The group's first comment was: "Was she real? Are there people like that?" However, a fortnight after the above visit, Letitia came back just, as we were about to finish. This is what she said:
"I thought I'd just pop in to thank you for the help you gave me. I have progressed and can now see flowers and grass, and I just want to express my grateful thanks for all your kindness to me. I have been visited by a little child, and she brought me a kitten, and this helped me to take my mind off myself, and with that, the pain seemed to ease and 1 was able to go into a reverie, and when I came to, there was my little girl guardian again: and now I have two kittens, two little white kittens. I am only here for a brief moment, and I am still not used to this sense of well-being. I thought you would like to know that you had assisted me and I do thank you. Goodbye."

CASE 17 UNABLE TO HELP

For over a year, starting in 2000, I was very concerned about a couple who were plagued every night by noises in their bungalow which prevented sleep. This had gone on for six years and had damaged their health. We exchanged many letters and phone calls, and I learned that the husband had had a previous marriage, which ended after he discovered that his first wife was a member of a group, which practiced Black Magic. Apparently he had returned home unexpectedly one day, and interrupted a ritual meeting of the group, whereupon his wife had placed a curse on him. The wife's brother, a teacher, was her partner in these sessions, and he had already been accused of improper behaviour towards children. I was sent photocopies of newspaper cuttings which confirmed details of this.

When we visited the bungalow, we talked to the wife and she confirmed all the details of the noises, which kept them awake at night. She said that they sounded as if a machine was scraping the floors of the rooms, making a loud, harsh sound, yet there was nothing to be seen.
We sometimes find that, in cases where there appears to be no spirit entity concerned, that a client is suffering from delusions, caused, perhaps from schizophrenia, in which case, medical, or psychiatric help is needed. In this case, the couple were so precise and sensible, that we had no doubt about

the truth of the problems they faced. They were a good living, Christian couple, who prayed for their persecutors and had already sought the help of the clergy, but all to no avail. A well respected, medium, from the local Spiritualist Church, had spent a whole night at the bungalow but had found nothing unusual.

John and Ron, could find no trace of a spirit entity when we visited, and Grey Cloud confirmed this, and I began to think that the cause of the trouble was, as the couple suggested, the evil influence emanating from the first wife and her group. Everything I could suggest, they had already tried in the previous six years, and they did not care to take the advice Grey Cloud gave them so, in the end, I felt there was no more we could do. The couple put the bungalow on the market, intending to move away, and I had to admit that we had failed, in this case, to solve their problems.

The Circle Changes

After seven years, Katherine, who had founded and hosted the 'Peace Circle' had to withdraw, and help her husband in starting a business. We felt we wanted to continue the work, if we were needed. We had been joined by another lady, Jean, a healer, and gifted trance medium, who allowed us to meet at her house. At this time, Judy, also a healer, developed the ability to work in trance. She seemed to be regularly used to help lonely, isolated spirits who had had no close human ties. Many were helped by bringing their animals to guide them to helpers or a house of their own. According to circumstances, we met at different member's houses at different times but we were told that the power needed was available at all them, and so it proved,

At the first meeting after Katherine left us, we wondered if the guides would continue to use us. Jean's guide spoke through her to encourage us:

Group: "Welcome friend. Would you like to talk to us?"
Guide: "I have not come for your help. I have come to thank you all. Thank you all for coming here today. We know that you have all had decisions to make, and from the fact that you are here, we are assuming that you wish to continue this circle"
Group: "Yes indeed."
Guide: "For that we thank you most deeply. I have already spoken to Jean today, and told her how much we appreciate the work that circles such as yours do. There are very few of you, therefore each circle is of great value in the work that it does, in helping those who are not as aware as

yourselves. By getting together, as you do, and giving your energy and tuning in, we are able to lead them to you, so that you can guide them towards the light, for want of a better expression. Without circles such as yours, it would be a very difficult task for us to do the work on our own, because they only relate at this time in their existence to the earth plane. They have no concept of anything beyond that. Therefore what you do in talking to them, the guidance you give them, just by listening to them, is of great value, and enables us to get close to them, so that we may then guide them to their proper place at this time. It is our wish that you do continue, but of course the choice is yours. Unless your heart is totally in the work you do, you cannot succeed. So we once again say thank you for what you have done and we pray that you will continue to do so.
God bless you all."

DO RELIGIOUS BELIEFS HELP AFTER DEATH?
CHAPTER 8

The field of human knowledge about the purpose of human life has been full of conflicting claims. Many religions have claimed to be the only true path to follow in this life so that a happy life beyond death can be achieved. On the other hand, sceptics claim that there is no afterlife, no supreme power and no purpose in human life – all is delusion! What is the truth? How do religious believers get on after death? How do atheists and agnostics get on? I think it best to present the evidence we have gathered in doing rescue work and let the reader decide where truth lies.

In many cases we do not know the religious belief of a person in trouble. Our object is, above all, to help him or her. In some cases a person will tell us, or make it clear what they believed, and in these cases we have to be careful not to upset them, or they may not trust us to guide them. We have helped a fair number of sincere Christians and Muslims and one Hindu. We have never, as far as we know, had to help a Buddhist or Spiritualist. The two following accounts were recorded when helping a Nun and a Salvationist after death. Because a particular atheist, Christian or Muslim needed help after death, I would not like to imply that other similar believers would need it as well. Where a belief encourages love and service to others, it can only bring good, even where misleading teachings postpone for a time the full enjoyment of the deserved happiness that spirit life affords.

Case 18 (R162) Helping a Nun.

Group: "I wonder if we can help you my dear".
Spirit: "Why? I don't know that you're a nun".
Group: " Well, we've helped lots of people. Tell us how you are feeling. Is it light or dark where you are?"
Spirit: "Just normal, I've been kneeling and praying but I haven't seen anyone for some time".
Group: "Would you like somebody that you used to know to come and help you and talk to you?"
Spirit: "How can they help me? I'm waiting for Mother Superior to ring the bell for lunch. I'm starving - I haven't eaten for so long. Me knees is killing me".
Group: "Well would you like to listen to what I say, because I think I can help you. The first thing is, do you realize that you've died – you've passed over?"

Spirit: "Good Lord".
Group: "Yes my dear, that's why you're in your present situation".
Spirit: "I know I wasn't feeling well. I had a funny feeling in my heart."
Group: "You know there's a lovely life waiting for you and if you'll listen to us, and take our advice, we can help you on".
Spirit: "But I was expecting to be welcomed into the arms of Jesus!"
Group: "Well that's a long story – (Spirit interrupts)
Spirit: "For the glory of God, I've been praying so long!"
Group: "Yes but that's something that will come much later."
Spirit: "Do you mean they're not telling me the truth?"
Group: "It's not that it's not true. It's just that it isn't true yet, you see. You've got some things to do first, so if you like to listen to us, and do what we say, it will help. Can you think of anybody who's already passed over that you were very fond of? Perhaps a parent or friend?"
Spirit: "I've not seen my parents for a long time, and they were a little bit on the rough side."
Group: "How about one of your friends?"
Spirit: "Sister Mary would be very nice".
Group: "And did she pass over?"
Spirit: "Yes."
Group: " Now what we want you to do, is to think very hard about Sister Mary, and ask if she will please come and talk to you. There's a group of us here, and we're all going to think of her as well, and I think if we succeed, she'll come and explain everything to you. Will you do that now? You've got to make a really big wish. Then we'll wait and see what happens. You can tell us if you see anything, or anybody comes."
      Silence
Spirit: "I seem to be in the middle of an orchard. Sister Mary used to do a lot of fruit gathering in the orchard. I never imagined you'd have orchards in the afterlife."
Group: "Oh yes, beautiful places, Paradise. Now we've got to find Sister Mary next."
Spirit: "Oh! She's there! She's hiding amongst the trees. I can see you Sister Mary, don't think I can't".
Group: "Is she talking to you?"
Spirit: "No she's just smiling."
Group: "You may hear her words in you're head".
Spirit: "We're just enjoying the joy of seeing each other. She's not saying anything yet, but then we were an order of silence on normal occasions, so we learnt to express our feelings by looking. We can stay as nuns for as long as we like."

Group: "Yes, good. Are you happier now?"
Spirit: "I'll just enjoy the peace in the garden. It's a change from all that time kneeling. My knees weren't what they used to be. I had so many years of kneeling. It plays on your mind wonderfully when you're praying. Your prayers become very heartfelt. You become aware that you really are a suffering sinner when you've been on your knees for quite some time." I'll go with Mary now and enjoy the peace, and I thank you very much for your help."
Group: "You're very welcome, could you tell us your name, my dear, your real name?"
Spirit: "Agnes."
Group: "Sister Agnes, God bless you. Be happy!"
Spirit: "And God bless you."

Case 19 (R163) Helping a Devoted Salvationist
Spirit: (singing loudly) "Marching as to war. I've a meeting to attend to."
Group: "Could I ask your name please?"
Spirit: "I'm not sure I should give my name to a perfect stranger."
Group: "Oh well, don't worry about it. I just wanted to ask you, are you happy? Can we help you in any way?"
Spirit: "That is not anybody's concern except my own. I'm in the Salvation Army, here to save souls. Does your soul need saving?"
Group: "I think it does. I think all our souls need saving."
Spirit: "We used to sing 'Onward Christian Soldiers', and sometimes it was very difficult to get people to join in."
Group: "Can I explain some thing to you, which I think you don't know, and that is, that you have died and passed over?"
Spirit: "Oh, don't be ridiculous!"
Group: "Into the next world, and this is why you are now speaking to us through the body of a lady -"
Spirit: "A lady?"
Group: "Who is allowing you to speak, so that we can come to your aid and help you."
Spirit: "But I am a lady!"
Group: "And this is a lady who is allowing you to speak to us, because we are still on earth, but you have moved over into the afterlife."
Spirit" "How come I haven't seen God then?"
Group: "You've go to wait a bit – you've got things to do first."
Spirit: "And where's Jesus? He should be here!"
Group: "That's all coming later."
Spirit: "Promises, promises, I don't know!"

Group: "Well, you see, you can't expect everything at once."
Spirit: "But I do – that's one of my unfortunate characteristics."
Group: "Patience is one of the virtues, and if you like to listen to us, I think we can be of service to you, and help you to a most beautiful place which is waiting for you. Now, it's a bit of a shock to realize that you've died, but you're a sensible person, and know that everyone has to die, so it's not so surprising, really."
Spirit: "I didn't expect it quite so soon."
Group: "Well, everybody thinks the same. What I would like to ask you is, is there anybody that you know that has passed over, who you were fond of, who you would like to see again?"
Spirit: "Brother John. He used to play the drum – the big drum. He went off not very long ago."
Group: "Well, if you like, we'll see if we can get him to come to you, and then you'll have somebody with you that you can talk to, who'll tell you all about this new life. I want you to make a big wish, 'Please could you come to me, Brother John?' Now, there's a group of us here, and we're all going to wish for Brother John to come to you. You make a big wish and we'll wait and see what happens."

    Silence

Group: "Keep wishing, you may see someone coming."
Spirit: "Do you think you could say the Lord's Prayer with me?"
Group: "Of course! (We all recited the prayer) Now Brother John, could you come to help, please? We're waiting."
Spirit: "I can see them all, with the drums, on the corner of that street."
Group: "Good!"
Spirit: "Perhaps, if I go and join them, I won't be intruding, maybe I can join in."
Group: "They'll be glad to see you – go and join in!"
Spirit: "Oh, it was a joy to join in. I've been longing to see them, and I thank you for saying the prayer with me. Oh, I feel so much better! The excitement of the Lord is upon me. I'll go with them."
Group: "God bless you."
Spirit: "I can go along with Brother John, now. We are going to do the Lord's work, even here. Thank you for letting me come. I'm sorry I was so rude. I didn't mean any harm. I'm a little bit on the bossy side. You get accosted by all sorts of strange men, and they make take advantage of the fact that you're a woman, so I had to sort them out and let them know who was who. Did I tell you my name?"
Group: "No."
Spirit: "Mary Maud."

Group: "We shall remember you, Mary Maud. Be happy,"
Mary Maud: "I'll say Goodbye."
Group: "Goodbye."

The spirit helper who spoke after these two ladies, said they were simple, well meaning souls, who had not found the higher self, within, but had followed a routine by habit, without much thought. They were good people, wrongly guided.

Case 20 (R114) Helping A Muslim.
Group: "What's your trouble friend?"
Spirit: "This is nothing like what I was told."
Group: "Did you expect something very nice?"
Spirit: "Yes."
Group: "And what have you found? Is it light or dark where you are?"
Spirit: "It is neither light nor dark."
Group: "Have you met any of your family?"
Spirit: "No. In other words, I am a miserable so and so."
Group: "I think we can help you. What were you told to expect? What was it you were looking for? Was it a Paradise?"
Spirit: "Yes, The Paradise. A lot of talk."
Group: "Is that the one in the Koran?" (He nods) I thought so.

Unfortunately, people don't go there right away. It's something one works up to – but they don't tell you that, do they? They say it is going to be there. There is a most beautiful Paradise, but you have to work your way there, and we can help you to do that. Now, is there anybody who's already passed over, that you would like to see – perhaps one of your family? Father, Mother?"
Spirit: "More so the father, than the mother."
Group: "Was your mother not very loving?"
Spirit: "Oh! She was loving within herself, but our way of life is different."
Group: "We'll have to see if we can get your father to come, and he can advise you of all the things that lie ahead. You must help us and we'll see what we can do. A group of us here are going to wish very strongly for your father to come and speak to you. You must help us, and wish for your father to come, Will you do this?"
Spirit: "I will, but I would like to thank that gentleman here from the spirit world, who has put the energy forward for me" (Grey Cloud).
Group: "He will appreciate that. Now let's think about your father. Make a strong wish to see him and then see what happens. Make a wish now!"

Group: Silence
Group: "Keep wishing."
Spirit: "Hmm."
Group: "Can you see him?"
Spirit: "Yes, and he has brought all the lights with him – a path to Paradise, or Heaven, whatever you like to call it."
Group: "Is he speaking to you?"
Spirit: "Yes, he is trying to explain that I am not, as you would say, going to Paradise."
Group: "He can take you to a nice place."
Spirit: "I think I may have done many things that were wrong."

    (Another spirit, now speaks through another medium)

Spirit (2): "It is your own anger that has kept your helpers at bay. If you had controlled your anger there were those there to help you, and lead you away from the darkness. We have brought you here so that these people may extend help, as this was the only way we could help you."
Spirit (1): "Yes, and that's why it was some time before I began to talk to you – because it was so strange to feel that I could talk."
Spirit (2): "We understand. We have all suffered and come to terms with things we have done wrong."
Spirit (1): "You see, we were told of this wonderful place from child up to manhood, but when things happen, there is nothing there."
Spirit (2): "This is the first step. You are on your way. There is something for you, but it is unfortunate that you were not able to fulfil all the instructions of your teachers. You only picked out the parts that were of interest to you."
Spirit (1): "Yes – that is so."
Group: "You are not the first to come to us with exactly this complaint – it is quite common. All, in time, will make their way to the lovely places."
Spirit (1): "This is not a complaint but a very big disappointment for me."
Group: "Will you go with your father now, he could take you?"
Spirit (1): "Oh yes, I will go with my father, I will come back."
Group: "Good. We should like you to come back. For now we say, 'God Bless!' and on you go."
Spirit (1): "I am sorry that I have been so much of a worry to you."
Group: "Thank you for that, but it is our joy to help people."
Spirit (1): "I will go."
Group: "Farewell. Be happy!"

Case 21 What a Churchman Finds.

Anthony Prescott.
AP: "How do you do? My name is Anthony Prescott. I used to insist on

being called Prescott, when I was alive, but things have changed now, so you may call me Anthony or Tony, whichever you wish. I have come to tell you my story. I am feeling a little peculiar first of all, being back in the body. I haven't done this before but I have been instructed before I came and I'm trying to do the things that they said."

Group: "You are doing very well."

AP: "Thank you. When I was alive I was very much the churchman. I was a businessman; I had a moderately successful business in the Midlands. I won't go into details, but it was a form of engineering, a small business and I lived in a nearby village, and was one of the people round and about that became, what shall I say, a benefactor of the church and supported it, and helped with money at times, when it was needed, and was appointed to various duties in the church. I had been brought up in it by my parents, they were very strict, they were of a - could I say - a Calvinistic type of Christianity in some sense, very, very severe and plain. I eased from that a little bit, and used to rather like to see some nice vestments and a bit of gold and lovely windows and colours – I rather liked that, in fact I donated a window to the church in my time, and I have continued my whole life going to church on Sundays, and on other days when it might have been necessary for something, not much in the week because I was too busy with my business.

But during that whole time of my life when I lived, and I was 67 when I think I died, I followed all the things that I was told to do, and I never really gave it much thought at all. I thought I was doing what I had to do for my afterlife. I tried to be kind to people, I had my business to run, and occasionally I had to dismiss people, because they did things wrong, you know, not quite... the word is Christian they say, sometimes, but you had to do it, if you had to keep your business. But I didn't think that I was doing anything particularly wrong, I was merely doing my business, which had to keep the family going, and it made good money, and I made sure that a certain percentage of it went to the church.

I had a window put in, as I said. I rebuilt an archway that nearly fell down. I helped with the roofing fund, in fact my name is up on the building as one of the benefactors of the church, and, do you know, now, I almost wish that this plaque was not there, because I was trying to buy my way into Heaven. I didn't really realize that that was what I trying to do, because I didn't give it much thought at all.

I went to communion, took the bread and wine, which wasn't really bread at all but a wafer thing, and I said all the prayers they said you had to say in church. I didn't do much out of church. I did when I was young because my parents were the type that said grace, and I had to say my prayers by my bed, as I expect some of you were made to do. I didn't understand them; I just parroted what I was told to say. I did the same in church and I asked forgiveness for me as a miserable sinner, but I didn't feel miserable at all. I had quite a good life, had a nice wife, two children who were adequately looked after; they became businessmen in their turn. I demanded that they went to church and went to Sunday school, now neither of them go anywhere near the church at all.

Well, my friends, as I said, I passed when I was about 67, and I had been retired a few years, and, as it happens quite often when you give up doing work you have been doing hard for many years, you do nothing for a couple of years, then all of a sudden (clicks fingers) - over you go, and my, was I surprised! I had been expecting to play golf for many years to come. The days of finding money for the church roof were over but I wasn't poor. I had all that I needed and I was going to enjoy my retirement with my wife. Still, up to the moment when I died, for all the things that I had been listening to in the sermons, I had never really thought about life after death. I don't know why I didn't, I just cannot understand it now. It was as if I compartmentalized it, and said the church has seen to all that, and I can get on with my life. I don't have to worry about that, so I didn't - never gave it a thought. I did my duty and I thought, well that's it. If there is anything, I've done everything I'm supposed to do. I'll go to the top of the queue.

I was suddenly struck down, they called it a heart attack, I don't know if that was exactly it, there may have been a weakness there, but we all die of the heart stopping in the end. I was actually at a function when I was rushed off to hospital. I don't think I ever arrived at the hospital. I remember suddenly realizing that I was watching a man being pushed along on a trolley through a hospital ward, and I seemed vaguely attached to him. It didn't dawn on me that it was my body for quite some time, because I hadn't really ever given any thought as to how one survived after death, and so I felt as if I was floating a little bit behind and above. Perhaps I wasn't quite gone at that moment, I don't know. They tell me this happens, and I could see lots of doctors and nurses rushing round and fixing things to the body, but it was no good. Now I am told this is quite commonly known nowadays and that when people do get resuscitated they call it something that I never heard of when I was alive. I believe it is called a, "near death experience."

Group: "Yes"

AP: "Well I think that this must have happened to me, but I did not return to my body. I wandered away for a while, thought I'd sit down somewhere and think about this, and I went into a corridor and sat down for a while. Nobody spoke to me, and I thought 'Well, here's me with a heart attack and nobody bothering', and then suddenly I saw two men coming down the corridor, dressed most strangely, in long white robes and they were talking to each other and walking down the corridor, they had bare feet. I always remember that, they had bare feet and they looked.... bright, that's the only thing I can explain. They looked more real than real ,and as they came near to me, one of them said 'Hello, old fellow, do you want to come with us then?' I thought 'Why should I want to go with these madmen in long white night gowns?' Perhaps they were mad ones who had escaped from somewhere. I couldn't make it out and I said. 'Who are you?' And they said, 'Well we've come to take you over to where you are going to in your afterlife'. Something like that, I can't quite remember."

'Well, you know you have left your body now and it's dead and finished. Now you have got to pass on, and we've come to help you.'
I said it was most interesting, and kind of you to come, what do I have to do? And they said, 'Walk along with us', and I got up and went in between them, and we walked down the corridor a little way, and then a most beautiful thing happened, it seemed to turn into this wonderful corridor of light going upwards slightly. We seemed to be going up, altogether, and these beings, all I can say is that they were like Angels, as they glowed brighter and brighter the more we went along, and eventually we came to a beautiful place, just like lovely parkland, can you understand that, beautiful parkland?

There were buildings and different things around, and people walking around, and we stepped out there and I looked at these angelic-looking beings, and they were beautiful. They said, 'Come and sit down over here, we are going to bring some people to help you,' and I sat down on this grass that was so comfortable to sit on, and they said, 'Have a rest for a while there,' and I had a rest. Then one of them called to a man who was nearby, and he came over, and I saw that it was friend of mine whom I knew had died some years previously, who I used to attend church with, and I was ever so pleased to see him. David, his name was, and I started talking to him, and when I looked round for these wonderful angel-looking beings, they had gone.

I started asking David who they were, and where we were, and what it was all about. He said I had to rest awhile, and he said he would stay with me, and he said 'If you want to you can lie down and have a little sleep.' I don't know, I did feel very tired so I lay down and had a little sleep. It seemed ever so funny to just lie down on the grass and have a sleep, not my style at all, like lying down on the golf course and falling asleep, but I did it.

Then I woke up again, and David was sat there, and, of course, I began to really take it in, it suddenly hit me, 'But if I'm dead, what is this sort of body' – not this one, this one, I can feel is a lady. Strange! I asked him all sorts of questions and he answered each one in turn. Now I understand that you know a lot about these things, you probably know the sorts of questions that were answered but I would like to tell you some of them for the sake of other people. They tell me there's some water here; the medium's mouth needs it. Thank you. Strange. That's better.

Well, my friends, what I would start to say is that beautiful as this place was, I had to find out in time that it was actually a place of quite a small amount of light because the realms on the other side – you go exactly to the point that is right for you, and where can you stand the light - if you can imagine that if you got into a very bright sun you couldn't bear it, so you stay in a place where you can bear it. Your soul, your body, your second body that you survive in, goes to this place.

I discovered that this was not the brightest of places although it seemed beautiful to me, and there was a wonderful church nearby. David suggested that we went into the church. We went in and there was a service going on, just as the services went on earth, and I said 'This is marvelous, just like home, this must be just like heaven.' He said to me that it was a sort of ante-room of heaven, you have to learn quite a bit yet, but your home will be here for a while, and this can be your church if you want.

I said 'Oh, marvellous', you know it was a very beautiful church; a lot of people must have given a lot of money for this church. He said 'We don't have money any more', so I said 'Well, it must have cost a lot, this church.' I couldn't get this idea of money and the church out of my head, do you see, because I had always seen it that way, I had no idea of any other way.

He didn't explain first but he said 'Well, if I were you I would just sit in the church and enjoy the church service.' Now it was just like a church service with all the same sorts of things and the prayers were the same, so I felt very much at home. I found some comfort in it because I was beginning to worry about my wife now. I don't know why, but it hadn't struck me at all about my wife, and my family, and I was beginning to worry. I found a lot of comfort in these words, which were so familiar to me. The only thing that was different was when the parson turned to give the final blessing, you know how they lift their hand up, and give the sign of the cross. Well a most wonderful light actually came out of his hand, and when it hit me I really felt something that I had never felt before. Can you imagine that? It was like a warmth hitting my heart and it felt healing and comfortable and I felt as if I was blessed.

So after the service we came out, and I said to David, 'I would like to go and find out about my wife,' so he said it was possible, but not quite yet, I had to rest a while longer. He would take me somewhere I could stay for awhile and he took me to his home. It was a beautiful home, lovely house, lovely garden, a beautiful, magnificent view. Peeping over the edge was the spire of the church. You could hear bells apparently from here, he likes it, and all the people round and about that we met, all seemed to be the same sorts of people that liked to go to the church. You knew they loved it; they were very fond of their church and attended the services. They didn't only have them on Sundays; they had them on other days as well. It was going on all the time, it was really nice.

We went back to David's house and he gave me something to eat and drink and I began to really think for the first time. He left me alone, sitting in a very comfortable chair looking at the view, I don't know where he went off to, he said he had something to do, and would I sit there. I suddenly said to myself, 'But this wasn't what the parson said in church at all, he never said anything about it being just like home, that there would be this lovely place with churches, this was not what they talked about.' When I came to think about it, what did they talk about? I tried to really pin it down, all those sermons that I'd heard and Bible readings, I'd read the lessons myself

I am sorry, I pause, I have to collect myself, I am not completely with it. Anyway, I began to think about that quite a bit, and when David returned, I asked him about it, and he explained life and death for the first time that I had ever heard. About the two bodies and how they separated and I said, 'Oh, was that what was happening to me when I was following the trolley?' and he said 'Yes'. He explained how you come away and live in another dimension that is very similar, but you live in your second body that was there all the time but you didn't know it, and that you could have all the things you wanted, if you deserved them. I think that was the way he put it, and he said that their whole life had been wrapped up around the church and that sort of thing, and this was the sort of area where those people came. We had our church and for as long as we wanted to, we could stay in this area, and I could have a house there, near him, and I would meet other friends.

I said 'What about my wife?' and he said, 'Well, until death us do part, my friend, you have parted from her now.' All of a sudden I had a very strange feeling and it was really peculiar, because I was sitting quite comfortably in this room, and I felt a tug, and suddenly I was in the churchyard of our church back on earth, there was a funeral going on, and it was my funeral. I stood at a distance and watched as they lowered the body into the ground. They were all crying, all in black, earth to earth thrown. My poor wife, who didn't seem as upset as I thought she might. My children seemed very sad, not quite as I imagined, but nevertheless they seemed quite sad, and I looked about to see if there was anyone I could talk to, and one of the angel beings was by me again, and he said,

'Yes, this is the burial of your body, it is no longer you, you have cast it aside and it goes back to the earth that it belongs to. The church is quite right in saying that. But here you are alive and you have somewhere to go and now these people here must continue their lives, your wife and your children, and if you really wish to come to see them you may come any time to see them, but they won't see you, because your church has forbidden it.'

I didn't realize that, you know, never thought about it. He showed me books and things that say they are not allowed to. He said 'Do you recall the text in the Bible about not suffering witches to live, and that sort of thing?' I said 'I remember hearing it read but I never sort of took in what it meant.' He said 'Well, they don't allow you to think that you could possibly contact each other once you are dead, so you are now on the other side of it, and you won't be able to do anything about it'. I thought that very strange, and rather sad, and I realized that I had an awful lot to learn, because it was very, very obvious to me that all of my life spent going to this church, and listening to these things and saying these prayers, had not prepared me for the truth of survival of life after death. I felt a bit cross that they had hidden it from me, can you understand that, my friends? In fact, I began to get rather het up, I began to think, 'All this money I gave to the church, the roof there, the glass, all these things, the porch that nearly fell down and it's up there because of me,' and I said this to the angelic being. He said that I had not given of my heart, only of my money. I had not thought of the people who worked under me, I had not really thought about my wife and my children very much, and those close to me. I thought that everything was taken care of by giving my money, and giving my time on Sundays to go and sit in the church and listen to the parson. It was not enough, my friends, there was nothing of the spirit given. I had given quite a bit of other money to charities and things, I had tried here and there, and had given people jobs by keeping my business going, and I had accrued a certain amount that allowed me to go to this area.

But I will tell you quickly that, after a time I began to tire of all these church people around me, and thought, 'Why aren't you realizing that what they told us there was wrong. Why are we continuing to do it here?' Eventually that query in my heart brought me the – I call them for you the angelic beings - they are some guides of mine. They call themselves,

guardians and guides of mine. They came back again and said 'If you don't want to stay here, you don't have to,' and I began to move on and I have moved on ever since, gradually. Occasionally, I go back to that church area in our dimensions, and try to find other people who are ready to move on, and I have moved on, and learnt a lot, but I wanted to tell you about my life as I went over, so I hope that was of interest."
Group: "Very interesting".
AP: "Thank you. I am going to leave now".
Group: "We wish you well".
AP: "Thank you. Perhaps I can come and tell you more another time?"
Group: "Yes please, we would like that".

PAUSE

Lee Ping:"I just returned for a moment just to say that I think this was an interesting story from those that do get trapped in any particular type of earthly idea, and how they think, by doing certain things and saying certain things, that this is going to ensure a place in heaven for themselves. This gentleman did do good. He was reticent in saying some of the good things he had done, which had earned him the right at least to go to this area, which was pleasant. Some of them don't land up in such pleasant places. I will leave you now and perhaps the other medium will be able to do some work.

Good afternoon and my blessings to you."

High Churchman in the Afterlife.

The position of highly educated churchmen when they find out the real nature of the life after death, is radically changed. Monsignor Hugh Benson was the son of the Archbishop of Canterbury, and a priest in the Church of England. He was psychic himself, and saw the people in the Spirit World but rejected this, as the temptation of the Devil. He wrote books condemning communication through mediums. In 1903 he joined the Roman Catholic Church and became a private secretary to Pope Pius X.

Hugh Benson returned after death to dictate through a medium two books, 'Beyond this Life,' and 'Life in the World Unseen,' in which he deeply regretted his two previous books and described in detail the wonderful life he had found in the Spirit World.

Another man, Cosmo Gordon Lang, Archbishop of Canterbury, commissioned a report on Spiritualism in 1937. The majority report agreed that the messages received, really did come from discarnate spirits, but the report was not published for another forty years. Cosmo, came through the famous medium, Leslie Flint, to say 'We are so grateful to people like you who come together in love, to serve - give up your time, to make the effort

to do the work of the Spirit. I achieved the highest possible place in the Church, but I hadn't the knowledge, the experience, that you people have. I know, now, that I was ignorant of what it was all about, If only the church would open its doors to this truth! You know Jesus was in communication with other souls that had gone before, as indeed were the Prophets.
My name is Lang. If you want to make use of what I have said, please do so. (Cosmo Lang has recently come through a medium in New Zealand (2006) to explain that he could not authorize the publication of that report at the time as he was only one member of a committee).

In the cases already described, such as Mark, the skier, and the lady who was 'Walking', their disbelief in a life after death seems to have caused them to be trapped. Letitia, on the other hand, had passed over, but her selfishness had landed her, like Wilf, in the lower astral realms, where other people were as selfish as she was. Because people like Mark, do not believe there is any life after death and, therefore, there is no one in that life to ask for help, their ignorance is their downfall. Once informed of the truth, they can soon progress. People in the Lower Astral realms only seem to be brought to us when they have already shown signs of wanting to progress.

A Bishop Returns.
In 1943 a young Catholic lady was so worried about my not having the true faith, that she persuaded to me to visit the Bishop of Sodor and Man for enlightenment. I arrived at the Bishop's Palace and was kindly greeted. The Bishop asked what was my problem in accepting the Church's teaching.

I said that I could not accept that the Church had Divine authority because I had been told that the verses 18 and 19, Chapter 16, in St, Matthew's Gospel, on which the Church's claim to authority rested, were not in the earliest copies of the scriptures, and that historians said they had been added later, to bolster the power of the Church. (Theses are the verses where Jesus said to Peter, "And I say also unto thee, That thou art Peter, and upon this rock I will found my Church; and the gates of Hell shall not prevail against it. And I will give unto thee the keys of the Kingdom of Heaven; and what thou bind on earth shall be bound in Heaven: and whatever thou shalt loose on earth shall be loosed in Heaven.)   At this point the Bishop suggested I had better leave, as they were not seeking converts.

Early in 2003 I had a messages from a medium who said, "I have a bishop here who simply says, 'I just want to say, that you were right and I was wrong.' I had only met three bishops in my life and it seemed likely to me that it was the bishop I met in 1943, who called in to correct a mistaken view. I wonder what I shall have to correct after I pass over?

THE SECOND GULF WAR
CHAPTER 9

Case 22 (178) Bombed in Baghdad.

On 27th March, 2003, an Iraqi lady came through in great distress. She was a mother, who, at first, could only weep and rock the medium to and fro in grief. She and her children had passed in the bombing. This is a transcript of the recording I made at the time.

Group: "Can we help you?"
Spirit: (Weeping) "My baby! My baby!"
Group: "We may be able to help you. We understand your sorrow.
Spirit: "The noise! The flames!" (She weeps again).
Group: "Tell us what happened."
Spirit: "The whole sky lit up!"
Group: "Did you know, my dear, that you have died and passed over?" (She weeps but does not answer.)
Group: "You've passed over into a new world and it can be a beautiful world, and we are here to help you, and tell you what to do."
Spirit: "I can't find her. A baby girl and a boy of four. A terrible noise and fire."
Group: "It's hard for you to understand, but you have passed over to a world which can be heavenly – like a Paradise. In a little while you may be able to see your children again. What we want to do is to get someone to come and help you and explain how you can see your children again.
If you listen to me and try to do what we say it will make you happier. We want you to think of anyone that you know that has died that you would like to come and talk to you. You could talk to them and explain your troubles. Who would you like to come?"
Spirit: "My Parents."
Group: "I think we can get them to come. Would you like to see your mother again?"
Spirit: "Yes!"
Group: "Think about your mother and make a big wish, 'Please come and help me!' Now we'll wait and see what happens."
 A pause
Spirit: "They're coming! I'm calmer now!"
Group: "Is your mother there? Tell us if she speaks to you. Is it getting lighter?
"Spirit: "Yes! There's a group of people here now."
Group: "Go! You can go to them."
Spirit: "They've got my baby!"

Group: "Go forward and take your baby!"
(She still weeps quietly and is given tissues to wipe her eyes).
Group: "Is your mother there?"
Spirit: "Yes! She's with a group of people and she's got my boy – we are all together now."
Group: "Wonderful!"
Spirit "Thank you!"
Group: "It is our pleasure, my dear."
Spirit: "Goodbye!"

Case 23 (R150) An Iraqi is Helped.
On the same date as the above, an Iraqi man spoke to us who had apparently been shot by his own side.
Group: "Welcome friend, Can you hear my words? We may be able to help you."
Spirit: "I hear your words but I don't know if I can trust them."
Group: "We are a group of friends who help people who are distressed, and we have helped many. Do you know that you have died?"
Spirit: "That is what I believe."
Group: "That is the truth – you have passed over - and we want to find somebody to come and help you, advise you and take you to a beautiful place. There is a wonderful place for you but you need some help. Can you think of anybody who you would like to come?"
Spirit: "The one I am thinking of, I would not like to trust his word again. It is very difficult. "Do you realize I have only just come to this side of life?"
Group: "We understand, now that you tell us. It is rather a shock."
Spirit: "It is rather a shock as you say when one gets it in the back from your own people, just because one has spoken one's mind."
Group: "We understand."
Spirit: "Pointless in having war. Absolute waste of people – your people – my people. Absolute waste!"
Group: "We agree, but did you know that nobody really dies? They just go into a new world."
Spirit: "I am still waiting for that world to show itself."
Group: "Perhaps you have heard of Paradise in the Koran. Now we've got to get you into a better place than you are in now. Who can you think of to help you?"
Spirit: "The only one I could trust would be my Grandmother. She has been in this world for some time."
Group: "Now we want you to make a big wish to see your Grandmother. Then we'll wait and see who comes! Tell us if anyone comes!"

Pause.
Group: "Can you see anyone coming?"
Spirit: "Yes!"
Group: "Are they talking to you?"
Spirit: "Oh, yes!"
Group: "Will you go with them?"
Spirit: " Yes! I will go with my grandmother but first I would like to apologise to your friend (John) in the upset he has felt from me.
Group: "We will tell him. He will know."
Spirit: "This war of your countries is not a good war, no wars are good, but I think it is a necessity. I know I should not be saying ill of my country. But this man has a twisted mind. He is a powerful man who lives on the hurt of others. So now I will go with my Grandmother. Thank you for your help."
Group: "It is our pleasure!"
Spirit: "There may be a few more who pass in this war who would like your help as well."
Group: "You could help to bring them here perhaps?"
Spirit: "It is rather early for me. I am sure there are those in the world of spirit who are waiting for them to realize where they are, and what has happened to them.

I myself have had a little of your beliefs taught to me, and I believe it is that which has helped me to come to you."
Group: "Thank you – that is interesting!"
Spirit: "Thank you again!"
Group: "Goodbye."

It is interesting that it was knowledge that helped this man to come for help so quickly. Even a little bit of knowledge makes a lot of difference As Billy says in his book, even if they've seen the film, 'Ghosts,' it helps the helpers to explain things to them more easily.

The Role of the Grandmother in Spirit Rescue.

When lost souls are asked whom they would like to come to help them, the most requested person is a grandmother. The bemused Arab, the baffled materialist, the rebellious atheist and the ill-taught Christian, all ask for the person they most loved and trusted in life, of those who have now passed over. In many, many cases, this is the grandmother, the one person who gave them unconditional love when they were little. Even in cultures where males dominate and women are condemned to a subservient role, the grandmother has a special place in the heart and memory, and is the person most trusted and most often requested to come and help.

Case 24 (R 227) The War in Sri Lanka. The Lost Boys

When acting as a rescue group we are rather in the position of a doctor, who only sees people when they are sick. We mainly talk to spirits who are in trouble. This does not mean that all spirits are in trouble anymore than it means that everyone is sick. As most ships at sea never need the help of a lifeboat, so most spirit people never need the help of a rescue group. We are just here for those who do need us

The next case is one where the medium saw a group of small boys. They had dark skins and looked terrified, clasping their knees, with heads down as they sat on their haunches. They looked abandoned and traumatized. One of them, an eight-year-old boy, then spoke through the medium.

Boy: "I want my mummy."
Group: "Can we help you?"
Boy: "She's gone away since I've been here."
Group: "Is there anybody with you?"
Boy: "Only the other children – there's lots of us."
Group: "Well, it's sad, but sometimes what happens is, you have to leave your mummy and she is ever so sorry that she can't be with you."
Boy: "I don't think she's sorry, she just left us. We haven't got our mummies, all of us, hundreds of us – it's not just my mummy."
Group: "Do you know anyone in your family who has died?"
Boy: "Yes, but they're dead, they're not here with us."
Group: "But we could get them to come to you and help you."
Boy: "I'm not sure I want them to come."
Group: "Wouldn't you like a nice granny or great-granny to come and help you?"
Boy: "No!"
Group: "They could help, you know."
Boy: "No!"
(At this stage we don't know what traumas these boys have been through. We are feeling our way.)
Group: "Have you got any of your friends who have passed?"
Boy: "Don't want them! Want my mummy".
Group: "Have you got any grown ups with you?"
Boy: "No. There's just these children."
Group: "Did anything happen to you?"
Boy: "Yes! Lots of war."

Group: "War, was it? I'm sorry, my dear. You see it may be that you got killed and now you're in the next world."
Boy: (more cheerful)"Perhaps that's why my mummy isn't here."
Group: "That's right. You see she's still in the world that you used to be in."
Boy: "But why didn't somebody come for us?"
Group: "Somebody should have come for you. We'll try and get somebody for you. It would be a good idea if you had somebody you were fond of who has already died, that would come and help you."
Boy: "I don't know anybody. I don't know anything about dying".
Group: "Didn't you have a granny or a great-granny?"
Boy: "I didn't get to know them."
Group: "Oh, I see. Don't you know anybody you'd like to come?"
Boy: "No!"
Group: "We'll see if we can find someone."
Boy: "Will they give me something to eat?"
Group: "We'll see if we can find another mummy, someone else's mummy, who would like to come and help you. What I want you to do, is to make a wish, and we are going to wish as well, for a nice mummy to come and help you. Your mummy can't come, because she's still alive in the other world. She can't get to you. She wants to, but she can't. There are mummies in your world, and we want a nice one to come to you and give you food to eat."
Boy: "They won't hurt us?"
Group: "No. We want someone who is kind, who'll give you something to eat and drink. We're going to make a big wish. Will you make a wish as well?"
Boy: "I see someone coming! She's very slim, she's got a dark skin, like we are, and long dark hair – doesn't look very old."
Group: "You can speak to her. Say 'Help, we want help!"
Boy: "I think she knows we want help."
Group: "Is she coming to you?"
Boy: "Yes!"
Group: "Does she say anything?"
Boy: "She did this. (He puts the medium's finger to her lips, as if to mean, 'don't speak') She beckons us to follow her."
Group: "She's going to take you somewhere nice. Are you going with her?"
Boy: "Yes, I've got to pick up some of the little ones. I'm not very big myself."
Group: "Do you know how old you are?"

Boy: "Eight".
Group: "Eight! Well, well! Get the little ones to come as well. You're going to be happy. It's going to be nice for you."
Boy: "Just not to be frightened would be nice."
Group: "Yes, away from the war. There is no war where you are now. Tell us what you can see."
Boy: "We can see she's got a long yellow thing on. She's picked somebody up, and we are all going with her. She says she's been trying to contact us, but we've been so frightened, she could not get our attention. She's got some mummy ladies. Oh, yes there's food - the children are running. She says we can stay here for a while, and no one will hurt us. She says we'll all have tea – we are in Ceylon. People are not supposed to hurt each other. We were taught not to hurt anything. It's very confusing."
Group: "Do you think you are safe now?" (Medium nods) "We wish you happiness, my dear. Be happy!"
Boy: "She says to say, 'Goodbye and thank you'".

    The medium said she did not get his name, but she could see many small dark-skinned boys. They were squatting on their haunches with their heads bowed. They were very frightened of something – they were very tense. The lady who appeared, was wearing a bright yellow sarong, almost luminously bright.

    It seemed very surprising that an eight-year-old, dark-skinned boy, could speak such good English, and that they were in Ceylon – now called Sri Lanka. However, all our spirit communicators agree that there is no time, as we know it, in the spirit world, and from 1798, Ceylon was a British colony and English was one of the official languages. Ceylon became an independent republic in 1972, and the name was changed to Sri Lanka, but it may have taken years for all the inhabitants to use the new name. Years, and even decades of our time can pass, and spirits are barely conscious of it.

    Over 100,000 people have been killed in the war between the Indian, 'Tamil Tigers,' and the Sri Lankan government, and it still continues to this day. These children may well have been victims of the, 'Tamil Tigers'. The boy seems to have been a Buddhist by his remarks, while the 'Tamil Tigers' are extreme Hindus, and may have carried out a 'Slaughter of the Innocents', as Herod was said to have done.

ANIMALS TO THE RESCUE
Chapter 10

In dealing with lost or distressed souls, it is important to sound confident and optimistic that help will, in fact, come. Sometimes, however, help seems slow in coming and the worried spirit may start to lose faith in this voice, which promises to help them out of their predicament. This is where, time and time again, animals have helped, leading the spirit to meet loved ones or other helpers, or simply being a companion again.

Dogs are frequently of help, but so are cats, donkeys and even parrots and hamsters. They all show their love for their former masters and mistresses by coming quickly when called upon. Four typical cases, out of many, are quoted below.

Case 25   (R164)   Animals to the Rescue (1) Two Dogs

Spirit: "What has happened?"
Group: "We may be able to help you. Just listen to what we say. Is it light or dark where you are?"
Spirit: "So, so."
Group: "I wonder if you realize that you have passed over? Did you know that?"
Spirit: "Yes."
Group: "Good! Have you made any friends or met people so far?"
Spirit: "No, I haven't seen anybody."
Group: "Good, then we are going to able to help you, this is our job. What I want to know is, is there anyone you know who has already passed over, that you were fond of and would like to see again?"
Spirit: "I was very much on my own."
Group: "Did you ever have a pet, a cat or a dog?"
Spirit: "I had several cats – I think two dogs."
Group: "Was one of them a favourite?"
Spirit: "That's difficult."
Group: "Would you like them both to come – the two dogs? Now what we want you to do is to make a big wish – wish to see your dogs again. Try and remember what they looked like! There's a group of us here. We're all going to wish the same, to wish your dogs to come to you. Now, will you make that wish? Then we'll wait and see what happens."
Spirit: "I feel they are there – I can't see them."
Group: "You will be able to see them later."
Spirit: "There's one large black, wooly one."
Group: "Good! Is he glad to see you?"

Spirit: "Yes! He was the cuddly one. There's one dog like him here now."
Group: "If you can see the dog, can you see the ground underneath the dog?"
Spirit: "Yes."
Group: "Soon you're going to be able to see scenery – lovely countryside."
Spirit: "Now they're here, I can take them for a walk, can't I? Oh! I think they're taking me for a walk."
Group: "Good! That's right, you follow them. They will look after you – and you can look after them."
Spirit: "Mmm!"
Group: "Follow them, they'll take you somewhere quite nice."
Spirit: "I had no idea this would happen. I thought that when you died, you died, and that was the end of it."
Group: "And that's why you didn't see them."
Spirit: "I was just being – nothing happened."
Group: "Because you couldn't wish for anything, you see. Once you wish for something you can have it. If you'd like a house, later on, you can have a house with your dogs."
Spirit: "As they say, 'This is the life'."
Group: "Good."
Spirit: "Thank you very much."
Group: "Off you go then. Be happy!"
Spirit: "I will."

Case 26 (R221) Animals to the Rescue 2.
A Case of Ignorance   Helped by Donkeys

This case shows how the belief that there is no life after death, and no possibility therefore, of reunion with those we have loved, can anchor one in a hopeless limbo, an existence of meaningless monotony and boredom. This lady had passed in bed, and remained there in her spirit body, because she did not realize that she had died.

Spirit: "Look, I've been in this bed, on and on and on, and I know I'm a bad tempered old woman, but I'm fed up with it."
Group: "I bet you are."
Spirit: "Nobody takes any notice of me, they're coming and going and doing things, and opening and shutting curtains. God knows why they're opening curtains, nobody's here except me, and I don't know what to do anymore. I've not moved anywhere, and all the family are still here. They don't take any notice of me anymore."

Group: "I think what has happened is that you've died and don't realize it. Your memory is still in the same house. We've helped lots of people like you. It's hard for you to realize it, but you've actually died, and we can get you into a lovely world, if you'll just listen to us. We've helped lots and lots of people because there's a brilliant world waiting for you. The thing is, you can get up out of that bed – you can just get up."
Spirit: "But nobody will see me! I keep getting up and nobody sees me."
Group: "Earth people can't see you anymore. So what we'll do is to get some people who have passed over to come and see you. Who have you known that you've liked and have passed over? Do you have anybody like a parent, a friend you'd love to see again?"
Spirit: (Tearfully)"Oh! I'd love to see Bill."
Group: "Now, we'll have a go to get Bill to come back we can do it you know. Now, I know it's hard to believe, but you'll have to trust us. Will you make a great big wish, 'Bill, please come to me! Talk to me!' Will you do that? We'll all make a great big wish, like a child, wishing for a present. Now we're going to wish, and please tell us if anybody comes."

Silence

Group: "It may get a bit lighter. Somebody may come out of the light. Tell us if anything happens!"
Spirit: "Well, I've got out of bed and I've gone to the window."
Group: "Did you ever have a pet a cat or a dog?"
Spirit: "Well, it might sound silly, but we did have some donkeys."
Group: "Did you? Did you have a favourite one?"
Spirit: "Well, I liked them all, but a favourite one was one with a blaze on its head like a star."
Group: "Do you know what his name was?"
Spirit: "We called him Pedro for some reason."
Group: "Now, while we're waiting for Bill, we're going to ask Pedro to come. Make a wish, Pedro, come on. We want to see you again. You might see them outside. Tell us if you see anything different."
Spirit: "I can at least see into the garden now, which is different."
Group: "Come on Bill! Come on Pedro! We want to see you."
Spirit: "The gate's opened! The whole crowd are coming in – 6, 7, 8."
Group: "You could go down and meet them."
Spirit: "Can I do that?"
Group: "Yes! You've got a new body. You can do anything – run – jump – walk! You've got a spirit body now. Now, down you go! See the donkeys! Can you feel them?"
Spirit: "Mmm, I can smell them. They're all warm."

Group: "Come on Bill, we're waiting. We want Bill. Remember what he looked like, what he sounded like."
Spirit: "Well, I was tall, but he was taller than me."
Group: "Concentrate on Bill for a minute. You've got your donkeys."
Spirit: "One of them is nudging me, pushing me along."
Group: "They might take you somewhere. Go with them."
Spirit: "They must have heard you. They're all running out of the gate now."
Group: "You go with them, wish yourself along."
Spirit: "I think he's coming, by the donkeys. I never thought to see him again."
Group: "You can live together again. Is he glad to see you?"
Spirit: "Mmm, He says 'Come on old girl' He holds me."
Group: "You'll be all right now, off you go."
The medium, Valerie, returned to say:
"It was such a pretty sight. All those donkeys swarming round this elderly couple. It was good to see."

CASE 27 (R203) A Cat Helps.
(The medium is weeping copiously, rocking to and fro)
Group: "Can I help you, my dear? Don't worry! All will be well. We are here to help.
(She weeps)
Group: "Can you hear my words?
(Medium nods slightly)
Good! That means we are going to be able to help you. Tell us your problem. Tell us what is worrying you?
(She weeps and mumbles incoherently)
Are you in pain?"
Spirit: "No!"
Group: "Are you frightened?"
Spirit: "Yes".
Group: "There's nothing to be frightened of because we'll get rid of all that for you and you'll be in a lovely place where you're quite calm and happy. If you can just manage to listen to my words, gradually you will feel better and better, and all your fears will go away. Tell us what is frightening you?
(Another medium speaks: "She is buried!")
What has happened, my dear, is that when we pass over, we leave our bodies and go off to a beautiful place, and we can get you into such a place, if you will listen to us. I know it is difficult for you, but you don't have to worry.

You're going to go up, up, up into the lovely light, and everything is going to be happy for you, for your spirit is eternal, it does not stay in the body. It has used the body and now it soars away to be happy. You are going to be free and happy.

What we want to do is to get someone to come and help you – someone you know – someone you're fond of. Do you know anyone who has already died, or passed over, whom you would like to come and talk to you? A parent, a relative, a friend?
Spirit: "My brother"!
Group: "Now what we're all going to do is, and there is a lot of us here, we're going to make a big wish for your brother to come and help you, but we want you to help as well, and if you can make a big wish, he'll come. What was your brother's name – can you remember?"
Spirit: "Mike".
Group: "Now, say 'Mike, we are calling for you. Please come and help!' Will you say this?"
Spirit: "Yes".
Group: "Good. You may find it will get a bit lighter. You'll see somewhere where it's quite light, and someone will come towards you out of the light. Now, make your wish! Tell us if anything happens.
SILENCE
Tell us if you see anything, or if you hear anything."
Spirit: (Now quite composed) "It's like shadows."
Group: "Good! That's a start. Keep wishing. Ask for help."
Spirit: "I can see black clouds, with sort of gaps. The darkness is going.
Group: Good! Soon it should be a little bit lighter. That will be the sign it has started."
Spirit: "I can see the sun shining."
Group: "While you are waiting, Did you ever have a pet which passed over? A cat or a dog?"
Spirit: "A tabby cat."
Group: " What did you call it?"
Spirit: "Tabby."
Group: "Would you like to call it? Say, 'Come and see me!' Think of him – what he looked like."
Spirit: "I can't see him but I feel something different."
Group: "He might brush against your legs."
Spirit: "Oh! I can see him now!"
Group: "Can you stroke him? Soon you'll be able to see him quite clearly, when you open your spirit eyes."
Spirit: "I can see him ahead. He's walking ahead!"

Group: "He's going to lead you somewhere. Just follow him."
Spirit: "He's leading towards the light. Now I can hear voices."
Group: "That's where he's taking you."
Spirit: "Oh! Oh! There are people. I can see them. They've been waiting for me."
Group: "See if you know any of them."
Spirit: "Oh! Oh! I can't believe it. My family. I never thought I'd see them again."
Group: "How do you feel now?"
Spirit: "Like I'm home again." (She weeps – overcome with joy)
Group: "Are they talking?"
Spirit: "They're cheering."
Group: "They'll look after you now."
Spirit: "Thank you so much. Good bye."

Case 28 (R173) Animals to the Rescue 4.
Freddie Can't get Home But a Dog Helps.
  The medium describes talking to a little boy of eight, who says his name is Freddy. He keeps saying 'I can't get home, I can't get home'.

Group: "I wonder if we can help you. We've helped lots of little boys. Can you hear my words?"
Freddie: "Yes."
Group: "Is it a long time since you went home?"
Freddie: "I'm hungry."
Group: "Yes."
Freddie: "I think I came out this morning."
Group: "Was that a long time ago?"
Freddie: "I don't know, I've lost track of time."
Group: "Don't worry Freddie. Do you think you could have had an accident? Can you remember?"
Freddie: "I'm usually careful on my bike 'cos Mum says I've got be careful. I don't know, I thought I was careful."
Group: "And what happened? Don't worry, it'll be alright"
Freddie: "Well there was this lorry (he bursts into tears) I don't know."
Group: "Now if you like to listen to us, we're going to get someone who can come and help you. I've got to explain something to you first. I don't know if you know, but when people die they pass over to a most wonderful world – Paradise or Heaven. I think possibly you've passed out of your body and we've got to get some nice people to come and help you. Can you think of anyone that you

known and you liked who's already died or passed over? Has your Grannie or Grandad died?"

Freddie: (In tears) "I want my Mum and Dad."

Group: "We'll see about Mum and Dad presently. Now, about Grannie and Grandad. Have they passed over?"

Freddie: "One Grandma died."

Group: "Right, what we want you to do is to think very hard about this Grandma who's going to help you. We want you to make a big wish, because, although you did not know it, Grandma that died is fine, she is full of life, she's well, and can come and help you, and she can tell you what to do. So will you think now about that Grandma that died, and say to yourself, 'Grandma, would you come and help me, and show me what to do – I feel lost?' – She'll come and help you. Will you make a big wish to see her? Now we are all going to wish as well, for Grandma to come. Now you've got to watch and wait and see if somebody comes to help you.

Now! Have a big wish for Grandma! Remember what she was like, what she looked like! It's all going to be all right. You'll be looked after.

      Silence

Group: Keep wishing, tell us if anybody comes. It may get a bit brighter somewhere, and someone may come out of the light. Say, 'Help me! Please help me!

Silence

Group: Tell us if anybody comes. It takes a little time.

Freddie: "Will she know me?"

Group: "Yes, she'll know you. She's been keeping an eye on you while you've been growing up. While we're waiting for Grandma, did you ever have a dog or cat?"

Freddie: (Less tears now) "I had a dog."

Group: "Do you know what his name was?"

Freddie: "I think it was Billy."

Group: "While we're waiting, wish to see your dog. See if you can imagine your dog coming to you. Think about your dog and look for it."

Freddie: "Mmm, I think I can see 'im"

Group: "Good."

Freddie: "Cos I can see a black dog running round and round and round, chasing its tail. That is what Billy used to do!"

Group: "Good. Is he near you, can you get near him? "

Freddie: "Will he hear if I call him?"

Group: "Yes, he'll hear you. Call him!"

Freddie: (More cheerful now) "He certainly listened. He's put his ears up."

Group: "Good. He's heard you. Now he might lead you to somewhere – to where your Grandma is."
Freddie: "He's running off and barking and coming back again – he always used to do this."
Group: "Now you go with him, he's going to look after you."
Freddie: "That's all right! I'll go with him."
Group: "He knows what to do."
Freddie: "Will he know my Gran?"
Group: "Yes. He'll lead you somewhere. Go with him! We'll keep listening to what you do."
Freddie: "He's playing. He was always full of fun. He's taking me over to some trees. He loves trees."
Group: "On you go!"
Freddie: "Along a path, I've got to run to catch up. He's going very fast (laughs) but he keeps coming back."
Group: "I think he's glad to see you."
Freddie: "He's so happy."
Group: "On you go with him."
Freddie: "I see some houses coming up down there."
Group: "Good! I think he's going to take you somewhere."
Freddie: "There are people cheering. They're saying 'Come on! Come on!"
Group: "Good."
Freddie: "Hmm. Lots of people. There's a table."
Group: "What's on the table?"
Freddie: "Nice things to eat. Cakes and biscuits."
Group: "I thought there would be."
Freddie: "It's like a garden. There's lots of houses."
Group: "Is anybody talking to you?"
Freddie: "They're all sort of hugging me. I don't know a lot of them."
Group: "They seem to know you."
Freddie: "Oh, I think my Gran's there! That's all right then. I think the party's for me!" (General laughter.)
Group: "Good! You have a nice party. Do you feel happier now?"
Freddie: "Umm! Thank you! Bye by."
Group: "Bye by."

WHO ELSE DOES RESCUE WORK?
CHAPTER 11

Besides the Spiritualist rescue groups, who work quietly in various parts of this country, others do wonderful work, as well. The Rev. Aelwyn Roberts, who has appeared on the David Frost Show, talking about this subject, was Vicar of Llandegal for 36 years, and Director of Social Work for the Diocese of Bangor. During that time he was the clergyman most in demand in his area, when people were troubled by ghosts. His first book, 'Holy Ghostbuster', was a best seller and, 'Yesterday's People', is doing well. When he first had to deal with a Ghost, he was lucky that a fine medium, or sensitive, who was also a research physicist, was willing to help. With another medium friend, the three of them became a famous team, spending hours in haunted houses all over North Wales, releasing earthbound spirits who did not know they were dead. He found no evil spirits but many of the old houses had many earthbound spirits still living in them, and they had to go through a number of them, before they finding the one that had caused a problem.

SPIRIT RELEASE   The Spirit Release Foundation
This organization, which is growing rapidly in the U.K., and has many members abroad, was founded by a highly qualified Consultant Psychiatrist, Alan Sanderson. He found that some of his patients, who did not respond to conventional psychiatric treatment, were in fact, possessed by spirit entities, who had not gone on to the Spirit World, but had taken up residence in a living human being.

Alan found a method of releasing these spirits, to the great relief of the patients, who were often unaware of any intruder. He finds that many patients and some alcoholics and criminals, harbour attached spirits, and can be helped, sometimes dramatically, by Spirit Release. One of Alan's most amazing cases has been published in the European Journal of Clinical Hypnosis, a case in which he released four spirits from the same patient, curing problems which had troubled her for years.

The Spirit Release Foundation runs training courses, and has a growing number of therapists, healers and doctors as members. Details can be found on the website at <www.spiritrelease.com>.

Spirit Release in the Churches.
The Bible has many accounts of spirit possession and of Jesus carrying out spirit release. In both the Church of England, and the Roman Catholic Church, most dioceses have a priest appointed as an exorcist to

deal with haunting and cases of possession. The methods employed are different, being mainly based on the idea of banishing the spirit to the lower realms, on the assumption that the spirit is evil, rather than assisting them to progress into the light. The work of these priests is further evidence of the reality of haunting and possession in this modern age. Bishop Hugh Montefiore, in his book, 'The Paranormal', explains that those with psychic gifts, which enable them to free earth-bound spirits, say that these spirits do not need exorcising. It is not the spirits of the dead, but only evil spirits, that need to be exorcised. Earth bound spirits have lost their way and need help. He says that for priests who do not have these gifts, the celebration of the Eucharist will usually be effective.

In 1972 a commission was set up by the Bishop of Exeter, which issued guidelines for the practice of exorcism in the Church of England. Because exorcism can be dangerous when carried out on a mentally ill patient, major exorcisms may only be carried out with the permission of a Bishop. The Roman Catholic Church has also issued revised guidelines for exorcism fairly recently, and there are over 200 exorcists appointed in Italy alone. These specialists have been appointed because there is a real call for their services from the public.

After the Reformation, the Protestant Churches dismissed the idea of Spirits manifesting, as all the dead were believed to be sleeping in the grave. However a distinguished President of the Methodist Church, Dr Leslie Weatherhead, in the book, "Wounded Spirits' gives a very good account of people being healed of possessing spirits by the intervention of a medium, who assisted a medical doctor after he had failed to make any impression on the suffering patient by conventional means.

Rescue Work in Other Cultures.

Rescue Work has been practiced in many traditional cultures for thousands of years. Shamans, Priests, Witch Doctors and Medicine Men, in many races, have done this work, as well as healing the sick and freeing people from obsessing spirits, the aim usually being to help the spirit to connect with the ancestors in the next world.

Many cultures have tribal rituals to help the spirit of the dying person to travel safely to the Spirit World. Because of these native traditions, and the general acceptance that there is a life after death, there tend to be fewer souls who are trapped or lost in these cultures. In the Tibetan, 'Book of the Dead', there is a detailed description of the stages of death, from the point of view of the departing spirit, and a precise ritual to be followed to ensure a favourable reincarnation in the next life. The eminent psychiatrist, Carl Jung, was so impressed by this Tibetan book, that he kept a copy by his bedside. He felt that the Buddhist writers had really penetrated the mystery of death.

In the monotheistic religions such as Judaism, Christianity and Islam, people were taught that there were only three options for the soul after death, Heaven, Purgatory and Hell. When, after the Reformation, the Protestant Churches dismissed Purgatory and taught that the dead slept in their graves until the end of the world, they were told they would awake to face the final judgement, which would send them to Heaven or Hell. The sufferings in Hell were so emphasized that people were terrified of death and what might follow. As Hamlet says, 'For in that sleep of death, what dreams may come? …….Thus conscience does makes cowards of us all'. Priests would tell their congregations to try holding their finger in a candle flame for as long as they could bear, and then imagine that pain all over their body, for all eternity, with no hope of relief, once they were consigned to Hell. No wonder, some Kings and Queens were reported as repenting in sackcloth and ashes, rather that be excommunicated by the Church, and so condemned to Hell and everlasting torment after death.

Terry and Natalia O'Sullivan, the authors of the book, 'Soul Rescuers', who have carried out Rescue Work all over the world, have found fewer lost souls in Hindu and Buddhist countries than in the western world. As the Rev. Aelwyn Roberts and his team found, almost all old houses in north Wales had several resident spirits, most of whom were perfectly harmless. This week I have heard of a house in Devon with six resident spirits. Only one of them caused problems and had to be moved on.

CONFESSION IS GOOD FOR THE SOUL

A good many of our clients are brought to us so that they can tell someone about things that they've done that are troubling their conscience, and are holding them back from progressing. Once they have confessed they seem to be free to get on with their lives in the spirit world. Let us look at some cases:

Case 29 (R44) Jack Confesses

"I am Jack. I've not been over very long. I did some very unkind things to my family, and I can't seem to get past this block. Somebody suggested about your group, that if I came along, you might be able to express this problem that I have. I didn't treat my wife too well, nor my little girl. I could give all sorts of excuses, it was my job, it was my health or it was my lack of money – there was always an excuse, but it was just sheer bad temperedness and a feeling that I was not in control of my life. I was made redundant at about forty. There did not seem to be any hope for the future, and I did put myself in the way of having an accident so that, in a sense, I committed suicide. I didn't actually do it – I didn't take anything, or shoot myself, but I was very careless and was not driving as well as I might have done - I drove too fast - and I caused my family a lot of stress from my death – and previous to that.

You think that if you die, you won't have to worry about anything, but I just want to warn everyone that this is not so, it continually goes over and over in your mind, because you can't go and comfort people in the same way – to put your arms around them and say 'Don't cry Daddy didn't mean it.'"

Group: "Are you seeing your wife and children now? Do you find yourself hearing them all the time?"

Spirit: "Yes! And I can't tell them that I didn't mean to hurt them." (He starts to cry softly)

Group: "Your feelings are what are drawing you to them aren't they? Have you seen any other people?"

Spirit: "People have been very kind to me, which, in a way makes me feel worse. How could I have been so horrible to my family?"

Group: "We can make it better for ourselves by working towards the light. Have people tried to help you?"

Spirit: "They have talked to me and said that my wife doesn't hold it against me, or my little girl. They understood the pressures that I was under, but it's the fact that I can't tell them – I can't hug them."

Group: "One day you will be able to tell them. It's a matter of waiting till that time, and how to cope during that time. There are people that will help. These people that come to help you, if you ask them, they will help you, temporarily to go to some places where you will feel a little bit better. At the moment your mind is trapping you where you are thinking, which is with your wife and child. To get over this, you're going to have to leave them for a short time. These other places are very nice and it would help you to get over it."

Spirit: (Sobbing)"You feel you shouldn't be enjoying anything because of the pain you caused somebody else."

Group: "I didn't say you would enjoy it – in fact they would probably give you work to do – other work – while you're waiting. They will help you to help your wife and children through their life. At the moment you don't know how to do it. First of all, you've got to let go of them a little bit, and let them live their lives, and you must live yours. Look round you now and see if one of those friends is there."

Spirit: "Yes! They are here. They said this is part of my healing process, talking to you. I do feel a bit better."

Group: "Ask them to take you to a comfortable place."
Spirit: "Trouble is, you don't feel you deserve to have a comfortable place."
Group: "I'm sure you did some good things in your life, things that mean you deserve some comfort. You'll be able to do some work of recompense."
Spirit: "They did say that work is a great healer."
Group: "That's right, it's when you pass over that that work starts"
Spirit: "That would be of some comfort."
Group: "Try to help somebody else. That'll be the first step."
Spirit: "It's when you feel so helpless, that you don't feel you've got anything left to give. You're just a pain to have around."
Group: "They'll show you how you can help your wife and child. It will be 'mind' help, not the physical help you used to give them"
Spirit: "I think part of the message, and part of the healing, is to say that anyone who is thinking of being careless of their life, which is valuable – just because you lose your job doesn't mean that your life isn't valuable any more – that, I think, is the main thought that has come to me since I have passed over, that most of the problems with humans is that they don't feel valued, because of this system, that if you don't have a job you're of no value. If you don't earn money, you're of no value. If you're not successful, you're of no value, so all I can say to everyone is, to value each other, no matter how small, or how low down the scale of things you are. If a thing has form, and has life, it has value.

God Bless you all."

Our next speaker, Helmut, had far more to confess, yet he found forgiveness and now sees how he was mislead by his teachers. Helmut was a high-ranking Nazi officer in Hitler's Germany. He confesses to actions which he now sees to be wholly wrong.

Case 30 (R22) Helmut the Nazi, Confesses.
Spirit: "My name is Helmut."
Group: "Welcome."
Helmut: "I was one of the chosen few. We were brought up to believe that we were God's gift on this earth. We were told that we were superior beings, and we believed it. We were given the best food, the best accommodation, and the superior teachings, regarded as necessary for our upbringing. We were told that we were the cream, the top, the, the highest, the most superior beings given bodies on this earth plane. Such false teachings, my friends. We had to find out the hard way.

We were taught to be hard. We were taught that other beings were inferior, and far below us in intellect, but we were not taught to love. When

I passed from my superior body, I found there were many things that I did not know, and one of those things was to care for others. I have still, unfortunately, a long way to go. As you can see I have difficulty in imparting an emotion other than 'self'. This has been shown to me, and I have seen it for myself. There is a great deal of work for me to do upon my spiritual body."

Group: "Why have you come?"

Helmut: "By allowing me to come, you are helping me greatly in my spiritual quest for knowledge. In allowing me to speak in this way, to say in a sense that I am sorry. I caused many deaths, I was in charge of many men, but I did not consider the feelings of the women and the children, other than to breed with the women to breed superior sons, and superior daughters to breed more superior sons, and they had to be fair-haired people. This land, this country, was made in the plans to become a breeding farm to supply the armies to take over the rest of the world, and all the inferior beings would be put to death All those with inferior minds or faulty bodies, they were to be disposed of, to create a utopia. What an illusion, to find that when you come to this side of the world, this side of life, that all beings matter, and the idea that you can be superior to another, other than in love, is a total illusion"

Group: "Could you say how you discovered that?"

Helmut: "I died while fighting, and for sometime I carried on fighting, until it began to dawn on me that I was fighting the same soldiers over and over again. And each time I thought that they had died or I had died, I got up again until I became weary of fighting and the thought came into mind, 'there must be something else'. That thought was my saving grace, because upon that thought, came a light, and in that light was a being so superior to myself that I fell to my knees. I saw the Christed one. I now realised (his voice broke with emotion) my arrogance and my need for humility. I threw myself to the ground and begged for forgiveness, and I was granted that forgiveness. I was taken to a quiet place of flowers and sunlight, where my soul recovered. I asked, on my recovery, that I do what I can (now in tears) to overcome that which I had done to so many. Forgive me friends! Take heed of what you do! Give thoughts to all those who suffer! Know that you will have to feel whatever you have done to others."

Group: "You must have done some good things as well."

Helmut: "It seems that my soul was good, and that my body was good, but the teachings put into my mind were false. Teachers brought me to this point, but there must have been something within me to have carried on, and come forward, and done that which I was taught to do. This was a trace element from a past life, which I had taken upon myself to face again, and,

it has, in a sense, brought me past it, so that seed is now burnt, and will never trouble me again. I thank you so much for listening."
Group: "We are pleased to hear and understand."
Helmut: "The closeness of the earth plane brings me to feel the emotion as I do, and all the memories flooded back."
Group: "This is probably the reason for coming.
Go forward in peace"
Helmut: "Thank you, and I say, Good afternoon."
Group: "We give you our blessing."

But What Happened to the Victims?
The Holocaust, a Victim's Story.   Of all the recordings I have, I think the most moving one is one made by a Jewish victim of the Holocaust. When it was played over the sound system in a cinema, there was hardly a dry eye in the place. We now have a copy of the minutes of the actual meeting at which plans were drawn up and orders were given, for the killing of six million men, women and children in Europe. Although the media, especially the BBC, have annual stories and programs in memory of the Holocaust, no one ever questions what happened to the victims after death. It is as if the western world were certain that death meant oblivion, and even the question of a post mortem existence could not be raised.

The spirit who spoke, gave his name as Jakob Mankowitz. He and his family lived in Prague before World War II, where they had a hardware business. When the Germans invaded, in common with many other Jews, Jakob was taken away one night and eventually ended up in a quarry in Austria as a slave labourer. He was one of hundreds, carrying rocks from the base of the quarry to the top. His family never heard from him again.

After nine months of brutal treatment and insufficient food, Jakob dropped the rock he was to carry. A warder struck him on the head and he died a short while later. In all his troubles, he had had in his mind's eye, a picture of his wife's face, the beautiful Hannah with the curly hair. Knowing nothing of the afterlife, at first he found himself in the dark but still conscious. Then, drawn by the face he remembered, he found himself earthbound, looking at his wife, now in a tiny hovel, but he was unable to communicate with her. Her hair was now grey, her face emaciated. Both her sons, David and Abel had been taken away and she was now utterly depressed and without hope.

Day and night he watched her, until the day the Germans came for her, saying she must leave to go to a factory where she would have work, and good food and clothing. With many others she was taken to a railway siding where soldiers forced them all on to railway cattle wagons, until no more could be pushed into each wagon. Again he followed as the train slowly made its way for three days and nights to a place called Auschwitz. They had no food, drink or sanitation, and some went mad on the journey. On arrival, the survivors had to jump down, and in doing this, Hannah sprained her ankle. She was classed as unfit for work and directed into the shower rooms and told to shower. After the shower, the gas taps were turned on and Jakob saw the bodies fall down – and then, to his amazement – he saw their spirit bodies emerge and rise up. At that moment, he suddenly became aware of something incredible. All around, were spirit beings, some dressed as nurses and doctors, helping and encouraging the bewildered spirits whose bodies had so recently died. A spirit said to Jakob, "Go to her! Hold her!" and he was able to seize her hand, and together they soared upwards, following the guiding spirits who urged them on. They arrived at an unbelievable place, a comfortable reception centre staffed by loving and welcoming compatriots. Here there were tables, beautifully laid, with delicacies and drinks such as they had not seen for years.

They had been so traumatized by the hardships they had endured, that their fear had not left them, but gradually they realised that were safe at last, as they chatted to friends and relatives who came to greet them. Jakob found himself a young man again and Hannah a young woman. They were given a room to themselves and slept in each others arms. They were told that their sons would soon join them and they would never again be parted against their will.

Classes were held to explain the new world they found themselves in, and it was made clear that they could if they wished make their way to even finer realms, if they could make spiritual progress. The hardest thing they were asked to do, was to learn to forgive the Germans for what they had done to them. It was explained that the German warders were themselves only cogs in the machine, trapped in a situation from which they could not escape.

This forgiveness was too much for Hannah to achieve, after her sufferings, but Jakob managed it, and with some others went to try to rescue Germans who were now in the lower astral realm. They also agreed to learn, so that they could try and communicate with an English group, in order to tell the world what their fate had been after their sufferings. They found themselves in a gloriously beautiful land with even more wonderful prospects ahead of them. Above all they said they wanted to tell Spiritualists that they did not really appreciate what a treasure they had in their teachings about the after life. "Our scriptures were not helpful!" they said, "They told us nothing about the real world we have here, where we have found peace and happiness. We say, ' Shalom' to all the world!"

The next tale is, sadly, a very modern one, one which many young people can understand.

Case 31 (R80)   Sandra Confesses.
Spirit: "My name is Sandra."
Group: "Welcome Sandra. Is there anything you would like to tell us?"
Sandra: "I have done something of which I am very ashamed."
Group: "It might be good for you tell us. Many of us have done something of which we are ashamed. We might be able to help."
Sandra: "I was taking drugs and I got aids, and this affected my child, and of course, I died and left the child unattended. I can't forgive myself, and so I can't expect anyone else to forgive me."
Group: "Do you know what has happened to the child now?"
Sandra: "She was adopted. Of course the illness is with her still. What a thing to do to a child!"
Group: "We understand your feelings."
Sandra: "That's one of the unfortunate things with the drugs scene, that your morals and your knowledge of right and wrong seem to fade into the background. You need the money to buy the drugs, so, if you can't get a job, you sold the body and then of course, you get the infection through sex with strangers. I did take precautions for quite a while, but I forgot – you tend to lose track of the days – whether you have taken any precautions or not, because of the need for the drugs and the baby was neglected anyway."
Group: "All this we understand, and many are in your situation but if we could just talk to you a little bit; life is eternal, you will have many, many more chances. One day you may even be forgiven by your child, because you will probably meet. What you do have to do is to see whether, in the future, you can make reparation, by helping somebody else who is similarly in trouble, which will bring you good Karma. So life is hard, it's difficult! Obviously you are ashamed. Shame does not create any opportunities. What you have to do is to say 'When I get the chance, I will put things right, as far as I can, and if I cannot undo what I have done, then I will help someone else.' Does this make sense to you?"
Sandra: "Well, in the long run, but I need to get beyond this overwhelming feeling that I am not good enough to do anything. Perhaps later, when I feel better, I can look after the children, but not until I can come to terms with what I have done."
Group: "We understand."
Sandra: "And forgiven myself. I suppose part of the process is to realize that I am still alive and the child will also be alive. I need to know more about reasons why we have to come to the earth plane in the first place."

Group: "That's right."
Sandra: "Why we need to suffer so much. We were warned about it, previously, but the pressure is extremely strong in the cities."
Group: "Of course."
Sandra: "And we need to be part of the scene. I suppose I need to able to stand alone. Facing this situation will possibly help strengthen my resolve, by going through the suffering and realizing that much suffering is necessary."
Group: "Try doing as much good as you can, then the feeling of guilt will disappear. It is the only solution – to do good."
Sandra: "I've reached the point where it is practically paralysing me. The point about doing good, is that people need to know that they can trust you, and that you are trustworthy. I have the feeling that those I might want to help would not want me near. I would need to ask permission first. People like me are being helped to realise the awfulness of their lives and the foolishness of that particular path. I had so many chances, but it is as though I had tunnel vision, and all else, apart from the acquisition of the drug, goes out through the window. The body so craves the substance. Not everyone gets so involved. If you have the type of body that seems to get addicted easily – I mustn't use that as an excuse – there's no excuse – it's just plain foolishness for which I am deeply sorry."
Group: "Do you still feel the craving for drugs?"
Sandra: "It is a craving, but they tell me it is a craving for love. I must learn to forgive myself in the same way that I would be expected to forgive someone else."
Group: "If you can remember that the ones above you love you, and they don't love you any less because you have been foolish. Their love is infinite."
Sandra: "But if I can't feel it, it is non-existent to me. I appreciate the thought."
Group: "Yes, but it's a useful bit of knowledge. You must go step by step by step, and you will gradually lose your feelings of unworthiness. You've made a start, because you've described it to us accurately, without self pity, which is a very good start."
Sandra: "I think I'll leave now."
Group: "We give you our love."
Sandra: "Thank you. Thank you very much. It is a start, admitting that I have the problem. Thank you."
Group: "Good bye and God bless you."

Sandra had spoken through Sheila. A strong male voice now spoke through John, another medium in the group.

Spirit: "I have been listening here, listening to our friend. In other words, I was just here, in case I was needed, but she has made much progress within herself, and in understanding the predicament she was in. She blames herself where there is no blame to be had. That was a case where there was a situation one could not get out of easily. Some of her friends were not as friendly as they were made out to be. In other words they were profiting by her misfortune, and it is the guilt of herself which she must overcome, which she will do very easily."

Group: "Oh good!"

Spirit: "I know there are so many questions in your minds that you want know about the spirit world. If you feel that you would like to ask a question, I will try to answer you."

Group: "Could we ask if you are one who does this work of caring for people such as our last visitor?"

Spirit: "I am, my friend."

Group: "Does the taking of drugs affect the aura?"

Spirit: "You mean does it have an everlasting effect on the aura? No, it discolours the aura, but does not break it. The colour can be mended. In other words, one can mend ones aura oneself. No one else can do it, only the individual affected."

Group: "Is the aura affected in the afterlife, or just on earth?"

Spirit: "Both, my friend."

Group: "Can healing not affect the persons aura?"

Spirit: "It can help rebuild the colour of the aura."

Group: "Does it help the actual person themselves?"

Spirit: "That is the main thing, to build that individual back to where it is supposed to be. Then, when the individual is being healed, so, the aura brightens."

Group: "Would you expect that individual to be given other lives in which to improve?"

Spirit: "That is entirely up to the individual. There are many arguments as to whether there is, or is not, reincarnation – I know there is – but no one from the spirit world will say to you, you must go back to the earth plane. It is up to the individual whether they want to come back to the earth plane, with all the anger, the feelings, the anxieties, again. I do not think I would want to come back again. I will leave you now. "

Group: "Thank you and good bye."

INTERESTING VISITORS
CHAPTER 12

Case 32 (R88) A London Gang Leader Confesses
    (This spirit had a powerful male voice)
Group: "I wonder if you would like to talk to us?"
Spirit: "Rather strange! I was here waiting before. Then the other gentleman poked his nose in, which I thought was rather rude."
Group: "So you didn't like being kept waiting?"
Spirit: "Do you like being kept waiting?"
Group: "It depends. Anyway we understand your position. Is there any way we can be of help to you?"
Spirit: "Well they told me, that if I came, you could help, but I am just wondering if you can."
Group: "Well, we've helped a lot of others. In what way do need help?"
Spirit: "First of all, I know that I am not on the earth plane, but where the devil I am, I do not know. I'm not here, I'm not there; I am just that bit in between."
Group: "Sometimes they call it Limbo."
Spirit: "Limbo! That's a dance, is it not?"
Group: "I believe it is, as well, but that's another meaning. I'm sure we can help you to get somewhere definite that you will enjoy. If you are prepared to listen to us, we have helped many others. What we would ask you to do, is to think of somebody who is not on the earth, but has passed on, that you would like to see – parent, relation, friend. Who you would like to come and get you."
Spirit: "I may like to see them – the point is, would they like to see me?"
Group: "Only time will prove that."
Spirit: "Only time can tell then."
Group: "Usually they are very willing to come and help, because they are not exactly as they were when they were on earth."
Spirit: "And I can assure you, I am not, because I was not on the - er- good side in the earth conditions."
Group: "We understand – now can you think of somebody who" (he interrupts).
Spirit: "There was one person who very much tried to help me, and he was a policeman – a very kind policeman - I know very well that he has passed, he has been –er- shot. But whether he would want to come and see me, after all the trouble I have given him in the first place? "
Group: "Well we shall see."
Spirit: "You see the difficulty?"

Group: "We've overcome this difficulty many times before, and I think we can do it again. The thing is, do you know his name? Can you visualize him?"

Spirit: "I can visualize him. Whether I can remember his name is another thing, because the memory plays tricks on you."

Group: "The name is not important, as long as you can see him in your mind."

Spirit: "Oh, I can definitely see him – I remember what he looked like – and his stripes."

Group: "Well, if you will concentrate your mind, and say 'I want to see him', we will try `as well, and then you watch and see what happens. You may be surprised, I hope you will."

Spirit: "We can only try, can we not? By the way I did not pass within the bars – do you understand? I was on the good side then."

Group: "Imagine you are going to telephone him."

Spirit: "He would be more likely to telephone me, because you know, I used to give him little informations for the police work, and that's why I did not pass within the prison walls – because of the people I used to give him information about."

Group: "You were what is called a snout, were you?"

Spirit: "A snout! That is what we used to call a cigarette. I think the proper name is informer, an informer for hand-outs, you understand?"

Group: "Let's all concentrate. We're going to concentrate – you do the same. We want the sergeant to come. See what happens. Think of him. Concentrate."

Spirit: (He sees the policeman)"It is a long time, Mr Harry! (To us) As soon as I see him I can remember his name. The only name I knew is Harry."

Group: "Is he there with you now?"

Spirit: "Yes, he is. He says I have not got the handcuffs this time. Oh, he is laughing! He was a very, stern, harsh, but a very fair man – very fair."

Group: "What's he saying?"

Spirit: "He is going over the things what happened in the past, and so on, and so on."

Group: "Will he help you now?"

Spirit: "Oh yes, I will go along with him, but if it was anybody else – no thank you!"

Group: "You can trust him, can you?"

Spirit: "Oh, I trust him – I was going to say - I would trust him with my life."(Laughter)

Group: "Well you are having a sort of life."

Spirit: "I am having a better life at this present time, than ever I had before. Life is so free, but when I was on earth, I was going from door to door, and looking round to see who was behind the door – life was hell."

Group: "You can be in heaven now; you are on your way. You go with him and he will show you all about it."

Spirit: "Yes, as long as he does not show me prisons (laughter) I have seen enough of those."

Group: "He won't show you those."

Spirit: "I hope not"

Group: "What is your name?"

Spirit: "Huh! What is my name? Oh dear, oh dear, oh dear, oh dear. I can't remember."

Group: "What did Harry call you?"

Spirit: "Everything bar my right name."

Group: "It does not matter."

Spirit: "What I can remember is, it was before the train robbery, before that time – just when your second world war was about to begin. At that time there was a lot of hanky panky going on – lots of little gangs in London – that's where I came from, London. There were gangs all over the place."

Group: "Were you part of one of those gangs?"

Spirit: "I am afraid I was leader of one of them, so you could see what style of life I had. So if I was leader, why did I push the leaders of the others? It was just to get power away from them. So there you are. I must thank you for allowing me to come and meet up with my friend. We are friends now, but we were super friends on the earth. He said 'I could see the good in you even before you realized it was there yourself'. I suppose he's what you call a guardian angel, yes? An angel in blue, with three stripes. I hate to think what the others are like. Well thank you so much."

Group: "You're very welcome."

Spirit: "If I am allowed to come back, perhaps I will remember my name and I'll tell you how I'm getting on."

Group: "Please do."

Spirit: "Yes, you know, they tell me you do so much work in this way, but a lot of them do not come back and thank you."

Group: "We don't expect it. It doesn't matter."

Spirit: "It does not matter what you expect. It is what I think should be done."

Group: "Well, we will appreciate it if you do. Enjoy your life."

Spirit: "I will definitely enjoy it now. He is telling me we have many places to go, many places to see, and many things that I can do, that I could not do before."

Group: "The abilities that you had on earth, you can now use, in maybe, a better way."
Spirit: "Oh yes! I can help people, instead of helping myself to other people's things. I will help people."
Group: "When they first come over, you can help people too."
Spirit: "Well I must say cheerio."
Group: "Cheerio. Good luck. God speed."

A general discussion followed as to why John had so many crooks and doubtful characters, like this gang leader, choosing to speak through him.

"I must be a crook myself," he suggested, but we agreed that as the only male medium in the home group, he was the natural choice for many men to speak through. We also wondered why so many of our communicators, especially the men, cannot remember their names, when they are first helped. Several of them said, 'Your memory plays tricks on you,' yet children, like Billy never forget their names, and some ladies give all their names.

How are we Judged?
Our next case shows that conventional standards of morality that we are brought up with are not quite the same as the spiritual standards which apply in the Spirit World, where kindness and love are the guide lines against which we shall be judged.

Case 32 Mattie, Lady of the Night.
Mattie: "It's a right old lark ain't it?"
Group: "Welcome whoever you are."
Mattie: "Matilda's me name, Mattie they used to call me. Yeah."
Group: "You've been before, haven't you?"
Mattie: "No mate, no, I haven't been here. No."
Group: "You're always welcome the first time. What have you got to tell us?"
Mattie: "Cor, Nice old place you got here, isn't it, eh? A bit better than what I used to live in I can tell you."
Group: "Where did you live?"
Mattie: (laughs)"Well I'm sure you can guess mate."
Group: "Well, whereabouts in London then?"
Mattie: "Well, I am from the East End but I used to go into the West End. I weren't a good lady, I weren't, no."
Group: "Piccadilly?"

Mattie: "That sort of way mate. (Group laughter) I didn't know about good at all. In fact I ended up real bad. That was the luck of the game as they call it. You live like that, you take the risk but it's a rum old life, I'll tell you.
But we meet all sorts, some good, some bad, some horrid. I thought I was for the high jump when I got over here! (Laughter) I really thought I was for the high jump, I mean I gave up all thought about church and that sort of thing. I just didn't think about it after I got into such things. I didn't mean to get into it, but to be honest, my mother was one. I tried not to, but by the time I was fifteen there weren't no other way. My mother took me up West, put all these clothes on me, and I was away. They call it a profession, and I was a professional. I knew what I was doing but it still ain't easy. There are times when you 'ate yourself. Down underneath, there's always this feeling that you're dirty. People look at you as if you ain't human. Anyway I got pushed to the other side, unfortunately, by this bloke what thought it was good to get rid of people like me. I was strangled."
Group: "Then what happened?"
Mattie: "Well I kept wanting to die. I could feel his fingers round me throat, I knew it was going to happen, and my head started buzzing and it felt as if me eyes was going to come out and then I couldn't feel anything. I kept thinking well hurry up and die then if you're going to die, for Gawd's sake, but I didn't. Then I see him running off and I thought, oh, that's good, he's gorn, I'll be able to get home again, and I sort of went about my business as you might say."

People didn't talk to me no more. Mind you I didn't feel that good after having that happen to me, I can't say I was in pain but I felt, Oh, you know, it was strange, I knew it had happened and yet I didn't feel as if there was any pain, that's the only way I can put it. I tried to talk to my girlfriend and everything and the next thing I knew she was screaming her ... I was going to say a naughty word then, her head off. (They told me I weren't to say none of my naughty words) and she was leaning over this body, and it were me, and I was dead. Somehow I knew I was dead. I didn't muck about, I've met a lot since that wander around and say they ain't dead. But I knew I was, because it was always a risk, I knew others it happened to, and somehow, I thought well that's it my girl, you're gone, what now? I mean here I was still walking on the streets where I'd always been. I didn't really know what to do. Then I sees this bloke coming towards me, he seemed a decent sort of bloke and he stopped and talked to me and I thought, 'Oh good, here's a customer'. (Laughs) Naughty! Then he says "Well that's all finished now, you don't have to bother no more about that".

"Well I've still got my living to earn," I said "No you haven't, you're dead and you know that, don't you?" I said, "Well I gathered it, but,"

I said "I don't really think, well here I am still on the streets. I've still got to carry on sort of thing," and he says, "No not here you haven't." "Come with me" Well I've walked with enough men not to bother about it, so I walked along with him, and I know this will sound daft but we hopped on a bus, only the bus seemed to take us into the country, which was lovely, and all these lovely places and people, I couldn't believe it.

"Ere," I says "where are we?" 'E says "Well this is where you are going to live now," 'E says "you don't need to worry no more, some of your friends are here," and believe it or not, quite a lot of the girls was there, yeah, and me old mum. I said I thought we were all so wicked we would, you know, go to the other place, not that I believed there was another place, but I didn't think there would be anything good, and he said "You see, most of you, most of you, lived your life in a way that was trying to be kind to people, you haven't got any hate in your heart really. You don't understand entirely. A number of times you were good to people, - he reminded me of some of the kids I'd given money to round and about, some of the old folk I'd given money to, 'cos that's what I used to do, you know. I used to go back to the East End, and I earned quite good money, and if there was an old Granny or someone that was short, like, I used to give them a bit.

And he says "No, you ain't going down there, you're going to be here," and I've moved on from there, and me Mum was there, and she had a lovely little house and we went in there and stayed there.

It's not an unusual story really it's just that I wanted to say that it's because you might look at people like me sometimes, you hear of them on the streets and things. Many of them are very kindhearted, you know. I know a lot of people laugh and joke and say a heart of gold, and all that but it's true, a lot of them are, but they're very kind. You've got to be a bit kind to do that job you know because the customers aren't always nice, some of them are very cruel and unkind to you, you put up with a lot, and then there's the rotten so and so's that batten on yer. So don't always judge by the outside. I think that's my message."

Group: "Thank you, we'll pass that on."
Mattie: "Do you want to talk about anything or ask anything?"
Group: "Anybody got any questions? Are you happy in your present life?"
Mattie: "I get a bid sad sometimes, I think I wasted my life. I try to go to school now and learn, and that sort of thing. This was some time ago when we were really thought of as something awful, I don't think it's so bad now, but they were thought of as really awful, this was after the first world war and in between that and the next one, but I died before the next war.

Well, I know it's not like any of you lot but I just thought I would tell you because maybe somebody who might hear some of your things

(tapes) might think that they ain't due for anything good, but it ain't always that, no matter what, it depends on the person and how they lived, and they can often find more waiting for them on the other side than them what they thinks that they're good."
Group: "We understand."
Mattie: "OK, I ain't going to stay long, I'll just leave you. Thanks ever so much for letting me talk to you."
Group: "Could you tell us your name"?
Mattie: "Mattie, Matilda. Mattie they used to call me."
Group: "Just before you go, have you got lovely jet black hair?"
Mattie: "Yeah, me Mum was a gypsy but settled down in London, she had no other way of earning a living, she was pretty and I had her hair, yeah."
Group: "Well, we give you our love, be sure of that."
Mattie: "Thank you, thank you for your work too, you don't know how it's appreciated on the other side. You do well."

Case 34 9/11 The Twin Towers A Victim talks:

On 20th September 2001, between 3 and 4 p.m., we were visited by a spirit, who spoke through one of our team of mediums. She explained that she had passed when working in the World Trade Center Building on the 11th September. I give below a transcript of the recording I made at the time of the spirit speaking through the entranced medium:

M: "My name is Margaret"
Group: "Welcome, Margaret".
M: "I was one of the English people who were killed. We know more or less what happened and I have just asked if I could come, just to give thanks for all the prayers that helped us, and to reassure you that there has been much help. There are a few wandering around, confused, but they have helpers with them - working with them.

It's just taking a bit longer with them, but it leaves us all, 'en masse,' in a very shocked state of mind, particularly as most of us are fairly young and have families. I don't think there is much I can tell you other than what you have seen. We have been talking to each other and sharing our experiences of what happened to each of us. Some have recovered fairly quickly, and were able to join in with the help - in the rescue of the people who are overwhelmed by their experience of coming to this side, and finding that they're not dead. We have found that by talking to each other, and helping, it is helping us to come to terms with the sudden change in our circumstances. We obviously have not gone on yet, to the place wherever we're going to settle. We've been told there's some other place we can go to but we need to be around for a while.

We are in another dimension - it's beautiful where we are - but we need to still feel we are in contact with our people - those we worked with - the families of those we worked with, and because of the mass sorrow, it affects quite a lot of them on this side. They are, some of them, experienced, and so are their relatives. We find the healing that has been given to us is helping us, and by being allowed to help as well, or to be around for a while, it helps us to overcome the shock. Do you understand this?"

Group: "We do. "Is there anything you would like us to tell people about the circumstances? Would you like them to know how you are getting on?"

M. "Well I'd like them to know that I'm not non-existing, that I do have a life, and that life will continue. It will take me a while to overcome my feelings of grief, myself, and I may have to go for a rest somewhere, but in the meantime I'm staying around to give help. Sometimes help is just sitting with someone while they're in a state of shock, or perhaps leading someone into the healing center, or leading them into a quiet garden, where they can absorb - or we can all absorb - the higher vibrations, away from that terrible, terrible accident - well it wasn't so much an accident, was it, but we thought it was at first. I was in the first one".

Group: "Were you - did you know you were hi-jacked?"

M: "I wasn't in the plane — I was in the building so we didn't really know what had happened. We just thought it was an accident of a plane coming in the wrong direction. It was only talking to the others, and the people who helped, who explained to us the situation.

I think people need to ask themselves, really - the government need to ask themselves - what causes so much hatred? Are they doing something that causes people to be so afraid? If you think about the different systems that human beings are brought up under, if it is a closed system and no alternate way of thinking is allowed in, these people have been brain-washed from childhood. That which is put into the minds of children is very hard to eliminate. So if people could bear in mind what they teach their children - if they teach children about fear, they help to bring up frightened children who grow into frightened human beings. If you teach them compassion for each other, you bring up compassionate human beings.

In a sense we can feel sorry for the men who took part in this act. They thought they were doing the right thing. In a sense they're not allowed to think too much for themselves. They have to follow instructions or fear being cast out of their belief system, and that is a fearful thing, also. Open minds, and open hearts is what is required here and I, for one, would not want anything - retaliation - in revenge. There are always people who get caught up in these wars - children again - and you continue to sow the seeds of fear and anger".

Group: "Did you know there was a life after death?"

M: "Well I believed there was a life after death, but I hadn't really gone into it in any depth - I just felt there must be something. I was not a religious person, I believed in a higher power and I put my trust in the higher power that there would be something for me round the corner. I trusted while I was alive that there was always something round the corner for me, and I still go on believing that."

Group: "Have you met anybody you knew that had already passed over?"

M: "No. These people who came to help, just emanated so much kindness that they felt like old friends. They took me in hand and said, 'Come on, Margaret, there's no need to hang around there for the moment. Just follow everybody else. Come and have a cup of coffee. It's amazing what a cup of coffee does. I think in England I was more for tea but you get in the way of the Americans here. I don't think there's anything else I'd better say at the moment".

Group: "Were you taken away before the actual accident or crash?"

M: "No!"

Group: "You actually experienced that, did you?"

M: "Yes, but there's so much smoke that within minutes - well less than that really - in some instances it was instant, whereas on the floor where the plane landed, you could say it was instant; for those on the different floors it would either be the masonry or the smoke would get you in a few minutes or fire. I think you'd have to speak to those individually. I can't say whether those in the planes went beforehand or whether those on the other floors went before the accident. All I can really say, is what happened to me, and one or two on the same floor as me. It's very confusing and when it goes black - dark - some people are rushing down the stairs and other people are falling down, and everything starts to crumble!"

Group: "It must have been terrible!"

M: "Yes, fortunately it wasn't very long. It's such a difference in the situation. It's such a relief to find you are not in pain and that you are away from it. I will leave you now".

Group: "Thank you so much for coming."

THE LANGUAGE PROBLEM

I have wondered how it is that a spirit who did not speak English when on earth, can speak through our mediums in English. At first I thought that only those spirits who could speak English already, were being brought to us. However, as French, Czechs, Germans, Arabs, Serbs, Japanese,

Africans and an Indian holy man, spoke to us in English, I looked for another possible answer. The spirits tell us that earthly language seems very clumsy and inadequate, as they get used to life in the Spirit World. This is because there they usually communicate by thought directly, which is why deception is impossible there, as each speaker knows what the other is thinking – not just what they are saying.

    I concluded that the answer is, that spirits pass their thoughts to the unconscious minds of the mediums, who turn them into English in the same way that they turn their own thoughts into English, and therefore it all happens quite easily. When a French Impressionist painter spoke to us in English, I asked him if he had to have spoken English when on earth to be able to talk to us. He said he did have some English, but he could have spoken through the medium anyway; it just made it a bit easier. The spirits do have a problem when the word they want is not in the medium's vocabulary, and therefore they cannot say it. Raynor Johnson said that he had to get Sheila to read certain books, so that she would know the words and ideas he would need, in a future talk through her.

Part III HAUNTINGS
GHOST BUSTING OR SPIRIT RELEASE?
CHAPTER 13

Case 35 (R60) OUR FIRST HAUNTING

By now, I was so used to talking to spirits, and advising them, when they were in trouble, that it seemed a perfectly normal thing to do. In fact, I often had better conversations with spirits than I did with people in everyday life. However, all this was done in a comfortable living room, in broad daylight, surrounded by a group of old friends. To me, dealing with haunted houses, and haunted people, was a totally different matter, quite outside my experience, but it was a matter that I was going to be increasingly involved in. One day, my very experienced friend, Ron. asked if I, and my trance medium friend, John, would help him, as he had received a call for help from a frightened young woman who lived in a flat, in a big house in Newton Abbot.

I did not take my tape recorder, but a notebook and pen, not knowing what was going to happen. The three of us travelled to Newton Abbot and a pale faced, anxious looking young woman answered the door to her flat. She explained that she was conscious of an invisible presence in the flat, which would switch the television on and off, and pull the curtains aside, as if to look out of the window. She could tell where the spirit was by its smell, which she found unpleasant. She was obviously distressed by all this.

We settled down and soon, John went into trance. A sad and melancholy look came over his face, and a male spirit started to talk through him He explained that he had owned this house in the 1920's and did not like it divided into flats with children running everywhere. He said he spent his time looking out of the windows. He did not like the modern car traffic or the new diesel trains he could see in the station nearby.

When Ron explained the distress he was causing the young lady, he was very apologetic. He said he knew we had come to move him on, and he was quite willing to go, as he had been there too long. When I asked if he would like to see his wife, who had died years before, he was hesitant, and explained that they had not got on very well. Ron was explaining that there would be a house for him to go to, when suddenly he said that his brother Tim had come for him and he would go with him. He apologized again for the distress he had caused and departed with his brother.

I went to call the young lady back into the flat, and she came with several other residents, who were agog to know what had happened. I explained matters to the group and we then left, saying that we could be contacted again, if there was any further trouble. On the way home, Ron told us of his previous experiences with ghosts, many of which had been grateful for help, while, one had been violent, throwing him to the floor.

Ron had now introduced us to a new field of work, which was to be very rewarding and occasionally rather frightening. We had no further calls from the young lady we had just left.

Case 36 (69) THE GHOST AT KFC

The popular press loves the expression, 'Ghost Busting' with its connotation of fighting the fearful unseen. As we know, this is a complete misunderstanding of the true position, which should really be seen as 'Spirit Rescue.'

Twenty staff work in shifts at a Kentucky Fried Chicken shop in Devon. For some time, the manageress had been puzzled as to why the female staff would not use the staff, 'rest room' upstairs. Then the fact came out that some of them had seen a ghostly, 'something,' and nothing would induce them to take their breaks there. The medium, John, was asked for help and he visited the premises and confirmed that there was definitely 'something' there. Friends offered to help, an appointment was made to visit, and at 6 p.m. on 13th January 1999, John, Ron. and I, passed through the kitchens and upstairs to the rest room at KFC. Ron. used a special instrument to test the area for electrical or geopathic stress. He found a fluorescent light malfunctioning under the stairs, and asked for it to be switched off.

I then arranged a recording microphone for John, who was seated in a large unlighted room, leading off from the rest room. The manageress and a male assistant peered through the doorway, to watch the proceedings by the light which came through the doorway.

I then offered a prayer for help, guidance and protection, while both John and Ron. tuned in to any spirit presence. After a short pause, John went in to trance and a voice began to speak through him. It was one of John's guides, Brother Peter, who in life was a monk at Buckfast Abbey. He assured us that no harm would come to John and said that the entity was a child of 13 or 14 years. Seeing that another spirit had arrived I said:

"Would you like to talk to us?"

Speaking through John the spirit replied,

"I've talked to so many, haven't I? When I come here there's people around; I talk to them and they run away."

"Do you think it's a bit naughty to make them run away?'

Spirit Boy: "I suppose it is, really. I notice you have one of the ladies here, and one gentleman. The gentleman is a bit sceptical. He thinks he's a big type of gentleman, and not afraid of anything. He, He! You see he has not seen me. He He! It is the ladies who have seen me. All I can say is I am deeply sorry but if you can understand that in this last war I was in rooms here. I lived here but I did not die here. I died when the bombs were falling and I suppose I lost my way. It is such a strange thing. Please, may I say to the lady, 'You can talk to me if you want to - you can you know, you can talk!'"

Manageress: "I can speak to you?"

Boy: "Please do!"

Manageress: "Do you keep coming back to play with the people that are working here?"

Boy: "He He! Which way do you mean play? Do you mean that I come back to frighten them?"

Manageress: "Yes!"

Boy: "No, I don't come back to frighten them. I just come back to have a look at where I was brought up', (turning to me). 'It is difficult for me to explain to this lady how things are in spirit."

M: "Perhaps we can do that afterwards. Now, have you met your mum or your dad?"

Boy: "No I haven't."

M: "Would you like to join them? They'd love to see you."

Boy: "I suppose that's why I keep coming back here in hopes that they would come back as well."

M: "Well, I think we should be able get you to meet your mum and dad! What we've got to do is wish! You've got to wish to yourself very, very, strongly, 'I wish I could see my Mum!' Then she'll get the call. We'll all wish together and then you can watch and see what you can see, and tell us it anybody comes. Will you do that?

Boy: "I will, but first I would like to explain to the lady that I am not English. I speak English, I was born in England, but of Polish parents."

Manageress: "Oh, yes."

Ron: "May I ask one question?"

Boy. "You can my friend."

Ron: "Do you know what year it is?"

Boy: "'This year now? Hmm. I know it is not the same year as the war was on. I believe that has been over some years."

Ron: "What I am trying to arrive at is, do you know what year you were buried?"

Boy: "Ah, it was the 40's, It was about then."

Ron : "Was it a bomb?"

Boy: "It was more than one bomb, it was a cluster - more than one. "Ah, it was 1943!"

Ron : "Thank you."

M: "Can we return now and ask if your mum can come? She can explain things, and help you on to a lovely place where you will be happy. Will you think about it now? Think 'Please could I see my mother?' Then wait and see what happens. You may see somebody."

There was then a long silent pause.

Boy: (Quietly) "Yes, it is her. It is my mother!"
M: "Good. Is she talking?"
Boy: "Yes, she is, in actual fact, saying that she has been looking for me as I have been looking for her."
M: "Will you go with her now?"
Boy: "I will go with her - Yes!'
Ron: "There is somebody else with her, isn't there?'
Boy: "Yes, there is, my friend, - that is my father - so that is proof to you my friend."
Ron: "Thank you."
Boy: "You see, before I do go, I would like to explain to the lady and gentleman that my other friend - he is what you would call clairvoyant. He sees other people round me at this moment, and he put me to the test when he said, 'Is there somebody else there?"
Ron: "It was not a test, my friend. Simply a matter of all the facts to be recorded."
Boy: "Perhaps I used the wrong word, - I give you my thanks."
M: "How do you feel, now?"
Boy: "I feel very much relieved, my friend, very much relief."
M: "Are they telling you what they're going to do?"
Boy: "Oh yes, we're going over to - Hmm – 'the other side."'
M: "Where you belong now. And you'll have plenty to do –people to play with -and enjoy yourself."
Boy: (Indicating John) "I think my friend has tried to explain to the lady what happens when people pass over but he did not have much success."
M: "It's difficult when people don't know."
Boy: "I will go now!'
M: "We give, you our blessing. We wish you happiness."
Boy: "Thank you so much for your help in putting me right after all this time. There are so many, in so many different places, who need the help. I must go. Goodbye! (turning to the manageress and almost shouting) You can tell your girls there will be no more shadows in the night. Goodbye!"

After the boy had gone, and John was back with us, we all sat down and Ron gave a talk to the two who had watched the proceedings. Neither was sceptical now, and both were interested as he explained that he had done this work for forty years.

"Was there any way of proving the identity of the spirit?" they asked. "Sometimes, yes, " Ron answered. After the last war many soldiers who were helped, were able to give their full names and service numbers and these were confirmed by the War Office, as correct.

We asked to be contacted if the spirit returned, as sometimes happens, and with many thanks from the manageress and a good tape recording, we departed via the kitchens into the street.

On Thursday 21st January I heard through one of the ladies that the, 'boy,' had not returned and all is now clear.

The following afternoon we started our 'rescue work' in circle. Through John, Brother Peter asked if we had any questions. At first nobody answered and he said,

"I did hear you raise a question before the meeting. This was, "Why could not the parents of that Polish boy contact him themselves? Am I right?" We agreed he was right. "The reason is," he said," that they were on two different levels and they needed the physical contact to help them make the link. There are many on the spirit side of life who do not know, realise or understand, where they are, and it is only through groups like this, that they can be helped, and if you will do this work we will help you as much as we can."

Case 37 (R73) A Mischievous Spirit.

Having received a request for help from a family in Exeter who for ten years had had problems with an entity, which made itself a nuisance, both in their house and next door; an appointment was made to visit.

At 7 pm on 7th April 1999 in the front room of the house, John, Ron., and I, listened, as they told us how the grown up daughter was plagued by the spirit, by day and night, until she was frightened and thoroughly fed up. Also that the son refused to sleep in the house when he came back to Exeter, but slept at a friend's house because of the spirit, which he had actually seen. Ron., long experienced in these situations, then used an instrument to check the rooms. As he did so he received advice from his own guide that they were going to be dealing with a determined and mischievous spirit.

Asking to be left alone in the front room, the three of us settled down, and I offered a prayer for protection. John tuned in, so that a spirit could speak through him if it wished to. I prepared to tape record all that occurred. The first voice that was heard was that of John's guide and friend, Grey Cloud, speaking through John in trance. The following is an exact transcription of what was recorded.

Grey Cloud: "I would just like to reassure you that no harm will come to my friend (John)."
M: "Thank you very much."
Grey Cloud: "I will be here, and if our friend does not wish to behave I will step in and not only step in, but I have other friends who will be more forceful than I. I know this does not really agree with your principles, but in that case we must have that extra strength to more or less forcibly eject this friend. So I will just stand to one side." A long pause followed.
Grey Cloud: "It is all right my friend, it is me (Grey Cloud). I am speaking to this young spirit (shall we say) and he is very reluctant to come forward – as I think you know, sir, but we will persevere and see if we can get him to come. I try to explain to him that he is not of the earth plane, but he is being of the stubborn nature – like all young ones really."
Another pause.
M: "Come along friend, will you speak to us? Speak up! Did you realise that you had died?"
Spirit: "Died?"
Ron: "You're well aware of that, aren't you?"
Spirit: "I am aware I died."
Ron: "Why do you cause problems for people who have not died?"
M: "When you die you leave your physical body."
Spirit: "You say I leave the physical body. How the devil do you think I am here?"
Ron: "You are here, purely and simply, because you will not travel on to the realm where you belong."
(Ron is getting advice from his guide as to how to tackle this spirit, rather in the way a newsreader gets advice from his ear phone).
M: "A beautiful realm is waiting for you. You have got stuck."
Ron: "You know this because you have been contacted before. You are well aware."
Spirit: "Yeah! I have to own up, in other words."
Ron: "Yes, own up. Also you have to realise that there are very powerful people on your side of the world, all around you at this moment. If you open your eyes you will see them around you."
Spirit: "I can, and I am trying to fight them."
Ron: "Yes – but you cannot win."
Spirit: "No – I tried last time. Did not win. But I managed to come back."
Ron: "Now you have brought a position upon yourself. You know what will happen unless you go where you belong."
Spirit: "Yes – my own prison."
Ron: "You will be confined, and taken to another realm and be there in confinement, until you decide to go forward."

Spirit: "Yes I understand that now. When you were speaking before I was listening, and you were right. I had that intent towards the younger lady, you understand?"
Ron: "Yes, I understand."
Spirit: "That is another thing I have to rectify and...."
Ron: "You don't overcome it yet. What you do not do by actions you do by intent."
Spirit: "That is right, my friend. That is what this gentleman who is stood here is telling me. I would not like to upset him as I have upset many people in this house."
Ron: "And not only in this house."
Spirit: "But also in the next house as well."
Ron: "And the other."
Spirit: "I am afraid I have traveled up to where the new houses have been built."
Ron: "Yes I know."
Spirit: "In other words I have been a – wandering minstrel – no that would be entirely wrong."
Ron: "A wandering spirit, my friend."
Spirit: "Yes, a wandering spirit has nowhere to go – but now I have somewhere to go."
Ron: "Yes, willingly or reluctantly."
Spirit: "I think it is going to be the former, my friend. I have had too much of the other – and you will not need to go anywhere else in this house, because this meeting will be sufficient."
Ron: "Good! Well, my friend, only good things are in front of you, because you will now face your future and know that it is your hands."
Spirit: "That is right, my friend. That is what this gentleman who is stood here beside the medium explained to me – that I go of free will. By doing that I do not have to go into the grey areas, but I will go to a slightly lighter one, and will have many friends. I do not know if you would like the lady to come, so that I can make my apologies to her."
Ron: "We will pass them on for you, as unfortunately the lady is not here."
Spirit: "I think that is better because (shall I say) I have left the fright within her."
M: "If you like to make your apology it is being recorded."
Ron: "She can listen to your words, we have a machine."
Spirit: "That is strange because when I was on earth you never had nothing like that, or that thing over there (TV set). I often turn that one on, which is very frightening for the young lady. But I do give her my apologies for frightening her – there is another word but I was no good with words."

Ron: "My friend, all you have to do is to look forward, and do not look back. The past is dead."
Spirit: "Like I am dead – but I am alive. I have as you say come alive again. I have left this material world with all its troubles. Now I am alive and can have the happy times with many friends who have gone before me."
Ron: "You will meet many friends, and as you progress you will have contact with your relatives as well."
Spirit: "You know this is a really happy release for me to be able to talk and realize what wrong I have done."
Ron "I have to tell you that your mother and son are listening. They will welcome you eventually to the realms to which you will progress."
Spirit: "Yes, and I do not think that it is going to be too long because, strange to say, I have a broken heart. You understand?"
Ron: "We understand."
Spirit: "But that heart is not what you call a material heart – but the heart of the soul. That is better. The heart of the soul is being mended. I will go with this gentleman who is stood beside me."
Ron: "We are happy for you, that you will do this."
M: "We wish you well."
Spirit: "I will, and I will not come back this time. And I know what you are going to say, my friend, you say that there are those who come back. I have come back before, but this time I am going for good."
M: "Thank you very much."
Spirit: "May I thank you for the opportunity which you give to people like me in so much as to get them away, as you have done with me."
Ron: "Then go, and make full use of the opportunity."
Spirit: "I will take the full opportunity now."
Ron & M.: "Blessings be with you."
Spirit: "And this gentleman is giving you his blessings too. And I too give you my thanks. I am really most sorry from my soul that I have caused all this trouble."
Ron: "Put it behind you and go forward."
M: "Peace, be with you."
Spirit: "And this gentleman is saying, will you please give this gentleman (John) some water after he comes back."
Ron: "We will."

We now called the others in and explained what had happened and thought all would now be well. If they wanted they could have a recording of the proceedings. If there was any further trouble they were to let us know. The next day they reported that all was well and asked for a recording. Later, when I delivered the recording, all was still clear.

Some days later, after a church committee meeting, a taxi arrived for one of the committee members. As he drove her home, the taxi driver said, "Would you like to hear an unusual tape recording?" On her agreeing, he started to play a copy of the tape I had made of the above rescue. He was the uncle of the young lady who had been attacked. He said, "I have been playing this tape to people all day."

Case 38 (R87 A Disturbing Entity and a Romantic Outcome.

I received a call asking for help from a family living in a flat in a large Georgian building on the outskirts of Exeter. The mother, a teacher, told us of an unpleasant entity making itself known in the flat- She would be woken at night by a male figure whispering in her ear, frightening messages, such as, 'You are very ill, and will pass tonight'. When her youngest child became frightened, she felt she must have help. Contact was made with a member of the, 'Spirit Release Foundation.' who referred them to us. We arranged to visit on 25th October 2002 at 7.30 p.m.

The teacher had discovered that the building had been used as a hospital for wounded soldiers during the 1914-18 War. Our party consisted of myself, as recorder, and John and Ron. as mediums. The following is a slightly shortened transcript of the recording that was made at the time.

Michael: "Good evening, Grey Cloud. Thank you for coming".
Grey Cloud: (Speaking through John). "We have one of our friends who is rather precocious".
Ron: "He has pains in his head".
Grey Cloud: "That is the condition in which he has been around the earth plane, my friend, a condition of war, but when I say, 'war,' it was through an injury which left that particular feeling with him. It is not the injury he received, which is making him like he is now. I think you will find he is trying to get his own way - trying to cause havoc - and, in your words, putting the fear of God up people."
Ron: "Ask him 'Who is Florrie?'"
Grey Cloud: (to spirit) "You must not be like that!" to Ron "Florrie is connected to this gentleman."
Ron: "Yes, I know, she is the stronger of the two!"
Grey Cloud: "Yes, it was with the rings. He was rather rude when you asked who was Florrie. He said,'"What the devil has it got to do with you?"'
Ron: "She is here. She has never been far away from him, she is telling me".

Grey Cloud: "He is saying he did not want to recognise her!"
Ron: "She is saying he won't get away with it with her".
Grey Cloud: "And he knows that. He is trying to draw away from us now, but we have friends around him".
Ron: "I am told he has to go with her".
Grey Cloud: "Yes".
Ron: "He has been very difficult and has been eluding the Angel of Light, for some time".
Grey Cloud: "That's true."
Ron: "I see there are also two more, here from your world. One is The Tibetan - he brings his light - and George is here. He comes with The Tibetan". (George Pratt and The Tibetan formerly taught an Exeter group in which Michael sat).
Grey Cloud: "Even the one we are talking of, has some of his so-called friends with him. That is why our friends have congregated together. I am positive that those two cannot break the bonds of love, no matter how hard they try".
Ron: "For sixty - four years, Florrie has stood by him - he has to acknowledge that".
Grey Cloud: "I think we should try and see if he could come and say a few words."
Ron: "Yes, please".
Grey Cloud: "Because I can feel the vibration from him as you my friend have been talking, so he is beginning to recognise Florrie, and the emotions which he is receiving and giving out."
Albert : (the spirit speaking through John): "Well, good evening. As I have been listening to your friends talking, it has given me back part of my life. But in giving me back part of my life, I, in a way, must relinquish the path, which I have been on. I am beginning to understand this. It is good for me to be able to use the vocal chords, which helped me to realize what has been happening. This may sound, 'double Dutch', to you. I know my dear Florrie, has been a cornerstone for me - but only for my stupidity - I did not realise it".
A Guide: (speaking through Ron) "Reach out to her!"
Albert: "God bless you my friend".
Guide: "Do not stand back - reach out."
Michael:"Accept her love!"
Albert: "Ah! My dear! I thank you for your undoubted love all these years. I ask your forgiveness, and the forgiveness of these dear souls, if I have caused any grief at all."
Guide: "You've always had it!"

Albert: "I will go to where I should be, with my dear Florrie."
Michael: "A beautiful place for you to go to."
Ron's Guide: "Go in peace! You are the beloved of your Father God! You have to prove nothing. Accept and go forth!"
Albert: "Thank you dear friends for those words of encouragement, which I take to the bottom of my heart, as I travel on with dear Florrie."
Michael: "You have our blessings!"
Albert: "We will go together!"
Grey Cloud: "Thank you my brothers, Once again we have joined our two worlds together.' There is still much we can do to try to do to put the love back into humanity. I will leave you now."
Michael: "Thank you once again."
Grey Cloud: "Once again I give my thanks to you, and to our
friend (John). I do not like to use the word, 'instrument'. It seems an unkindness - I prefer to call him friend. So, Good -night, and God Bless you in your work, in whatever way you do it for Spirit."
Michael: "Our thanks to George and, The Tibetan."
Grey Cloud: "Yes".

Time and time again, we have noticed how a spirit which has been indulging in very anti-social acts, annoying and frightening innocent people, will suddenly apologise, and even thank us for rescuing them from the evil they were quite happy to indulge in before they were forced to look at what they were doing. Are they just pretending to have changed their ways? I feel myself, that as their centre of consciousness changes from the earthly ego to the spiritual self, the change is automatic and quite genuine. However, if they manage to return and get up to their old tricks, I shall be proved wrong. I've not heard of such a case yet.

DESPERATE APPEALS
CHAPTER 14

Case 39 (R92) Driven From Home.
A Terrifying Episode for a Young Family

In early February '04, I received a 'phone call from a young woman, asking for help. She said her husband, Bill, was terrified by the happenings in their house. When she was out, he went upstairs to see to the baby. When he returned, all the furniture in the room was moved diagonally across the room, and the photos taken from their places and piled on top of one another. When he went to the loft, he saw the shape of a figure up there, which so startled him that he lost his grip and fell to the floor below.

I asked to speak to Bill, and he confirmed all that his wife had said. On Friday, 6th February, at 7.30 p.m., I went to the house with John and Ron., and we sat round a dining table in a beautifully furnished living room. The children were in bed but a kitten was playing on the settee. Joan and Bill retired to another room.

I set up my recorder and John went quickly into trance. A voice spoke through him; it was that of his guide, Grey Cloud. He said, "I cannot detect any entity here". Ron said, "No, there is nothing out of the ordinary here". Bill had said that the atmosphere in the house had changed recently. For two days, the house had been back to normal – a lovely, family, homely atmosphere.

We said that perhaps the entity had been frightened by our coming, and, after saying that they could contact us again if they had further trouble, we left the house at about 8.20 p.m.

The following Sunday, I was leaving Church at 4.30 p.m. when the 'phone rang. It was the young woman, Joan, again. She said, "Help! We are desperate! We have left the house. We could not stay".

She said they had had four adults and five children in the house when someone went to the bathroom and found the word, 'KILL' scrawled on the mirror in soap. The next visitor to the bathroom was horrified to find the pet hamster's dead, mangled body, lying in it's own blood in the washbasin. It had been taken out of its cage and killed. Later that night, fearing for their children, they decided they must leave the house. Bill went to the loft to get a carrycot for the baby and saw two fierce, red eyes, glaring at him. I said we would come as soon as I could arrange it, and put the phone down. It rang again. It was Joan, giving the phone number for the house where they were now staying. I was concerned at the young couple having to leave the lovely house and also for our safety when we visited. I had never heard of a spirit entity that could move heavy furniture and kill an animal. In the previous year, when Grey Cloud wanted to contact me about an interview arranged with a TV programme maker, he went to a medium friend of mine in London, and got her to ring me up. As I am not a medium myself. I decided to ring her up for advice. She answered the phone and immediately said that Grey Cloud was there, and that he said that the entity was a spirit called Timothy who had a deep resentment against his parents, who had passed on many years ago, in the days when men wore top hats. He said we would be well protected and need have no fear. Two other guardian spirits would restrain Timothy so that he could be dealt with. When John came to pick me up, to go to the house, he said that Grey Cloud had also contacted him to say that a powerful spirit with two lions would be there to overawe Timothy and hold him in place.

We arrived at the house at 7.30 p.m. on February 10th and the two young people had plucked up their courage to let us in, and stay in the room with us. This time the entity was present. As before, I set up my recorder, John went quickly into trance, and Grey Cloud spoke.

Grey Cloud: "Good evening, my friends".
All: "Good evening".
Grey Cloud: "Good evening to you, young people. You do not have to be afraid. You can talk to me as much as you like. I will not bite you, I promise. (He laughed)
Grey Cloud: (To the spirit) So you think you are clever!"
Ron: "We come to bring light and love".
Grey Cloud: "It is all right, my brother. I was just talking to this gentleman. He seems to think he is, what you call, 'top man'. Hmm. I was just asking him if he would like to talk to you. He has refused once. He has nothing to be afraid of, so why doesn't he talk? It's because he knows he's in the wrong – very much in the wrong. (To spirit) All right, try and get past me. You have another one of us here, as well., and that's why I don't think you will get past, not with these two lions. (To group) I will see if I can coax him to talk".

An interval of quiet followed.
Spirit: (Angry and gruff) "What you doin' 'ere?"
M: "We've come to help you friend, to see if we can make your life better".
Spirit: "I don't need your 'elp!"
Ron: "If that is so, why did you hide yourself the last time we came here?
Spirit: "To show you I'm cleverer that what you are."
Ron: "Is it clever to frighten people?"

Spirit: "Huh. No, not to frighten people, no."
Ron: "You did!."
Spirit: "I was just trying to show 'em what power I got, what I could do - what I 'ave done".
Ron: "Yet all you were doing was creating fear".
Spirit: "I'll tell you what, mate, I'm a bit fearful of what's rahn me nah".
Ron: "Why?
Spirit: "E's too bloomin' big, that's why!"
Ron "You see, if you use force, if you use power, you induce a power greater than your own".
(The telephone rings.
Spirit: "Blimey, what's that?"
Ron: "Just a moment".
M: "It's gone now".
Spirit: "Oh, it's one of them newfangled things – isn't it? Didn't 'ave 'em when I was down 'ere".
Ron: "You heard – if you use force, you induce a greater force!"
Spirit: "Yes – I bin proved that, aint I. Not only that Indian chap, but one over there with two great lions – I don't like them for a start. You keep them away from me!"
Ron: "There's no need to fear. What's your name?"
Spirit: "Timofey".
Ron: "Do we call you Tim?"
Timothy: "If you want".
Ron: "OK, Tim. How old are you?"
Timothy:"What, when I kicked the bucket? – in my forties – you know, between forty and fifty. I gone past forty but ain't reached fifty."
Ron: "When was that?"
Timothy: "Cor, blimey, a long time ago. It was when the men wore them big 'ats - not the clothes like they wear today".
Ron: "So it's probably nearly a hundred years ago."
Timothy: "Yeah – give or take a day or two – mustn't be too precise, must we".
Ron: "We don't want to be too precise, but the main thing is, before you kicked the bucket, as you call it, you had a family, who had gone before you".
Timothy: "Yeah, that's right. I 'ad my dear sister – she went before me – she went with the ole fever."
Ron: "But, you know, they've come here tonight – two ladies, one much older, then the one you're speaking of."
Timothy "Cor, lumme! And that one went before me sister, didn't she – and that's me mum."

Ron: "And she wouldn't be short of clipping you round your ear."

Timothy: "Oh! She'd do it now, wouldn't she? Yeah! 'Course she would."

Ron: "She's learnt a lot, and she says you'll learn a lot. You didn't go to school much, did you?"

Timothy: "No, I used to minch off with it. I used to go down the river bank, looking in the ole Thames' mud. 'Ahd did I get down 'ere then?"

Ron: "You were drawn down here to an easy target and the gentlemen round you now, are keeping you here. Now, would you kick a babe in arms?"

Timothy: "No, I wouldn't!"

Ron: "Essentially, that's what you've been doing. You've wasted a hundred years."

Timothy: "I got a lot to make up then."

Ron: "You've got to make up for the fear and distress you caused other people. You can't escape that."

Timothy: "Not now, I can't, not with these two 'ere."

Ron: "Now, you've got an Indian standing with you, a big Indian."

Timothy: "Yeah, I know."

Ron: "If you turn and look behind him, what do you see?"

Timothy: "Huh. Oh crumbs! 'Allo mum! Cor!"

Ron: "You didn't think you'd see them again."

Timothy: "Cor! She ain't 'alf waggin 'er ole finger at me again.. Oh, blimey, I'm in for it! I tell you one fing, Mr., I used to 'ave a fear of 'er. Cor blimey!"

Ron: "Are you prepared to go with her. Now, if you look across, there's another gentleman standing there, he looks like a Chinese."

Timothy: "Yeah."

Ron: "Who's with him?"

Timothy: "There's another Indian by 'im."

Ron: "And whom do you know that's just behind him?"

Timothy: "Oh dear! I ain't seen 'im for a long time. That's me ole dad."

Ron: "Why do you think they've come?"

Timothy: "To take me by the scruff of the neck."

Ron: "To take you to a better place. There is a place where they have been for more than a hundred years."

Timothy: "Do you mean to say they've been waiting all that time. Cor, she must 'ave the patience of Job"

Ron: "Exactly. And you haven't helped."

Timothy:"Sheesh! What the 'ell can I do?"

Ron: "The first thing you can do is to apologise to these good people that you have made to fear.

Timothy: "Oh, crumbs. It's going to be difficult. Isn't it?"
Ron: "No!"
Timothy: "I tell you it's difficult!"
Ron: "It isn't! You did not want to cause them fear, did you?"
Timothy: "No, I didn't. Then why the 'ell did I do it?"
Ron: "Because you were still living the old life – putting on a bold front."
Timothy: "Can you two forgive me?"
Joan and Bill; "We can try."
Ron: "You see this is their home now. These houses weren't built when you were here."
Timothy: "No, they wasn't."
Ron: "So you are intruding in their home."
Timothy: "That other Indian just told me – all right, I'll try and say the word. I don't know what it means – is it retribution? What's that mean?"
Ron: "It means you get back what you give out."
Timothy: "Oh, cor blimey, I'm in for a rough time, you two, in't I?"
Ron: "Unless you change your ways. The first step is to be prepared to go to another place from where your mother, sister and that other gentleman came. Now they are not able to punch you on the nose, much as they might like to, I'm sure."
Timothy: "Dad would."
Ron: "They don't want to. They want to take you with love. The other is a much happier place. Will you go with them?"
Timothy: "Yes, because they've both changed their ways to what they was when they was down 'ere. I often used to get a beating."
Ron: "There won't be a beating because that body has gone, but you, the real you, is much more alive than ever. If you go with these people that love you, they can help you and bring you to a much more happy and contented way of being."
Timothy: "Yeah. All right, then".
Ron: "Now, if you turn, there's mother and sister, both there."
Timothy: "Yeah, I'll go."
Ron: "And you're going to go with them.. Mother is telling you. She will take you and help you, until you have gained enough strength to stand on your own".
Timothy: "Now, I'll tell you somink else – the chap with the two lions, he's 'opped it. 'E's gone. (turning to Bill and Joan) So I won't bover you two young people again."
Ron: "I shouldn't try it!"
Timothy: "I'm not going to – not with this one – there's two Indians still 'ere. Not with them two!"

Ron: "Go, and take the hand of your mother!"
Timothy: "Well, I can't get enough words to tell you how sorry I am!"
Ron: "We understand".
Timothy: "I know you two do, but I want the other two to understand, as well. (To Bill and Joan) Just for a little joke, you can turn round and say you spoke to a spirit person."
Ron: "They possibly will do, but they wouldn't want to make it something to laugh about."
Timothy: "No! I know. I'm going to say, 'Cheerio', to you now – all right?" I'm going now, but before I go, the Indian has told me to tell you that they've put a padlock round this house, so nobody else can come – not even me. I want to say, once again, I'm awfully sorry. I'm sorry from the bottom of my heart."
Ron "That's a beginning."
Timothy: "Cheerio!"
Grey Cloud: "I will stay with my friend for a little while until all has quietened down."
Timothy: "I only do it for a bit of fun, don't I?"
Ron: "Did you young people understand what that was all about?"
Bill: "Yes"
Timothy: (Still here) "That young gentleman can go and have a pint now. But only have one – not like you usually do, one, two or three!"
Ron: "You shouldn't be watching him!"

Ron: "He was a bit of a wide boy who was attracted by your light. He was not here the last time we came – he did a bunk, but tonight, having cornered him, he couldn't get out. He was a braggart, but he'd had a hard life. You should have no more trouble. You're protected now. Can we have a glass of water for the medium, please?"

Accustomed as we are to going to a doctor for help, it was a change to be asked for help from a young G.P., who had a problem that medical training had not prepared her for.

Case 40 (R83) A Doctor Asks for Help
In November 1999, I had a call from a lady doctor called Dr Mac. She and her fiancé were doing up a three storey house in Heavitree, Exeter. Her fiancée D, had seen something so upsetting he could not bear to be in the house alone. I visited the house with John, and we heard further details. The young man had been looking into a built-in cupboard on the third floor, when he saw the apparition that terrified him. In the cupboard he saw two

forearms, joined at the wrist by a rope. They were just above waist height and there was no sign of the rest of the body. He was so horrified, he left the building and it was some time before he could enter it again.

We asked to be left alone in the room. John tuned in, and said there definitely was a presence. After contacting Ron, a very busy man, I made an appointment for the three of us to call and tackle the problem.

On the appropriate evening we called and settled ourselves in the room on the third floor. I arranged to record the proceedings while the other two 'tuned in'. * The first sound we heard speaking, through John was a husky breathing, and then, spoken slowly:

Spirit: "Difficult to talk."
Michael: "Well done!"
Ron: "What is your name?"
Spirit: "Jac-ob."
Michael: "Welcome, Jacob."
Ron: "Do you know where you are?"
Jacob: "I have re-coll-ection of where I was."
Ron: "Where was that?"
Jacob: "Not very nice place, if you can understand."
Ron: "But it was not here?"
Jacob: "No, not here, but not very far away."
Ron: "I understand, and what was that place?"
Jacob: "It was a place of execution."
Michael: "We understand" (The old Heavitree Gallows had stood nearby).
Jacob: "Rope around neck. I think that is why I now find it so difficult to talk."
Ron: "We understand that. Why were you executed?"
Jacob: "In that time one was executed for minor things."
Ron: "And what did you do?"
Jacob: "In those days, I stole horse. You understand? Stole to gain money by selling horse."
Ron: "Can you tell me what year that was?"
Michael: "Or who was on the throne? A Queen?"
Jacob: "It was in the reign of Queen Victoria, when she was in younger years".
Ron: "Before she was queen, or after she was queen?"
Jacob: "Before. Before she was actually queen (1837?) I feel I am making it rather difficult for you".
Ron: "No, that's quite alright. Do you know, at this moment, where you are?"
Jacob: "I cannot say for certain, but all I can really try to explain to you, is that I want to get away from where I am."

Michael: "We can help you do that."
Ron: "Put your hands on your tummy, will you?"
Jacob: "Here?" (He puts them on John's tummy).
Ron: "Yes."
Jacob: "What is reason?"
Ron: "You were a very small man. You did not have big tummy. Can I suggest that is not your body?"
Jacob: "Yes, yes, I can understand that. It feels very strange."
Ron: "OK. Now, do you understand how you can be experiencing what you are experiencing in a body which is not yours?"
Jacob: "Hmmm. That is rather difficult to explain."
Ron: "Yes, but do you agree with me, that is not your body?"
Jacob: "I agree with you, Sir, that this body is not my body, it is someone else's body."
Ron: "Right."
Jacob: "So if I come to conclusion, I am not of your world, as it is now, so therefore, if one has any brain, whatsoever, I must be somewhere else."
Ron: "In your day, they would say you were dead."
Jacob: "Yes – and that is what I believe."
Ron: "Now, when you are dead, you leave your body, but because you can think, you make a condition of your own. You said you want to get away from this place."
Jacob: "That is very true, Sir."
Ron: "But that place is a creation of your memory."
Jacob: "But sir, forgive me, if I am dead, how is it that I can still talk to you?"
Ron: "That is what I am coming to now. Your body was destroyed, but nobody can destroy you! You are a soul. Have you heard that?"
Jacob: "I think I may have heard that in my younger years."
Ron: "Well you are a soul, and that lives for ever, but now we have to get you to see somebody who you know is dead – your older brother. You know he died before you did."
Jacob: "Oh yes, he definitely did."
Ron: "Will you look slightly upwards, and to your right? What do you see?"
Jacob: "I see my brother, who is taller than I."
Ron: "You know he's dead. Do you notice something else? He's in a light?"
Jacob: "Yes, he seems to be in a glow."
Ron: "Now, put your hand towards him, and take his hand. Will you go with him?"

Jacob: "I will go, most happily, with him."
Ron: "Because he will help you to create another reality."
Michael: "A different world."
Jacob: "And this is where I wish to go to. From many teachings ago, when one was young, and there was religion, one was taught these things, but as one grows, one has thoughts of ones own, and disbelief, but now I know I must go with my brother to meet my other brothers who are with him as well. I will go with him as he is now beginning to turn and wants me to go with him."
Ron: "Then go in peace and with our blessing!"
Jacob: "I will go, as you say, in peace"
Ron: "Then go into that better world that's now yours".
Jacob: "May I please thank you for all the trouble you have gone to, to help me on my pathway."
Ron: "Thank you."
Michael: "It is our pleasure, but we thank you."
Ron: "It is also our joy to do the work which we have."
Jacob: "My brother has just reminded me I must give my apology to the gentleman I upset."
Michael: "We will let him know that."
Jacob: "I will go with my brother."
Ron: "God bless you."
Jacob: "Before I go with my brother, I must thank also that Indian fellow who was here."
Ron: "No thanks are necessary. They do this for love."
Jacob: "It is only right we give them recognition."

After this episode. the doctor and her fiancée visited Ron at home, as the young man needed counselling. Ron explained that, as he was a natural psychic, he would have further experiences of this kind, but this did not reflect on his sanity, only that he had a gift which he could develop if he chose, to be of help to humanity. The doctor sent us a card of thanks and a donation to church funds.

Case 41 (R228) Two Ghosts and a Suicide
Some friends of ours deliberately let some properties they own to people with mental handicaps, who cannot easily find accommodation elsewhere. The wife, who was naturally psychic, knew there was a ghost in one of the flats, but was not worried about it. Her husband, who had had a bad fright as a boy, did not care to be in the flat on his own. However, both were shocked when they found the lady tenant of the flat, hanging from the

banisters. Obviously she had committed suicide. They felt the tragedy keenly and also were kept very busy dealing with the official side of the affair. They had feared to ask for help with the ghost before, for fear of upsetting the tenants, but now the flat was empty, they felt they could not let it again without getting help to move the ghost on.

We were asked to help, and on 23rd April 2003 we visited and were shown the apartment. After I opened in prayer, Ron and John 'tuned in' and I prepared to record the proceedings.

This account is taken from that recording. An authoritative voice spoke through John that I did not recognize, so I thought of him as a new guide.

New Guide: "First of all my friends, there is one gentleman here and one younger person. The young one, we are not particularly bothered about, but, saying that, we must let her have her say. She says she is from a generation back, before your last war, when the clothes people wore were entirely different to what they are today. She is rather persistent about that. She says she only came to have a look round. She does not mean to scare people. If she does, it is not intentional. She has no connection to the other person, the one who has to be, shall we say, chastised. She is sorry if she has upset anyone. She explains she died of diphtheria and this upset her self-confidence."

Michael: "Is she happy?"

New Guide: "She says she is now entirely happy and it is a wonder they have not seen her little black cat"

Ron: "Has she seen her uncle John?"

New Guide: "Well," she says, "I think I have', and you know she has a very cheeky smile on her, as much as to say 'Yes I saw him, but I could not believe it.'"

Ron: "Only I believe her Uncle John has been trying for some time to get her to see him."

New Guide: "This is perfectly true, but, she says, 'I could not believe it was really him.'"

Ron: "Well he has been trying for many years."

New Guide: "Yes."

Ron: "Was he not her Godparent?"

New Guide: "Yes, he was. She says he was trying to educate her in scriptural matters on the earth, and things went wrong somewhere. Perhaps the illness affected her mind."

Ron: "There is a difference in his attitude now."

New Guide: "She says she will go with her Uncle John now, with all the lovely flowers he used to grow, and still does grow. Well, we will let our little friend go on her way now, and we will see if -. Yes, all right – she is just reminding me that it does not matter what he has done, he is still a gentleman. She wishes you all a very pleasant evening."

Michael: "We hope she will be happy."

New Guide: "She will now. Not only has she got her Uncle John, but some of my young friends as well."

      A long pause followed

Michael: "Would you like to talk to us?"

Spirit: (very low and aggressive) "Don't need your 'elp!"

(This was followed by heavy breathing and muttering)

Ron: "You killed, but you not intend to. Would you like to tell us about it?"

Spirit: "It was not very nice."

Ron: "It was in a drunken stupor."

Spirit: "Of course, when one is in such a state, things go haywire."

Ron: "But you are not in that state at the moment."

Spirit: "I was going to say, my friend, I know I am not in that drunken state now, but I still get that feeling."

Ron: "This is only the shadow. It is not the present reality. This is the trouble, but it is in the past. The past is gone. We do not make judgments."

Spirit: "No, I am beginning to understand that."

Ron: "But what we would like you to do, is to move on and begin the work of making reparation."

Spirit: "I understand what you are saying now, but had you spoken to me before, I would not have understood one word, because my mind was upside down." (He chokes and coughs with emotion)

Ron: "What is your name? Your Christian name is all we need."

Spirit: "My name is such a common one. It is Thomas."

Ron: "You have done one thing. You have acknowledged who you are. Can you now acknowledge Rose?"

Thomas: "That was the lady I forgot, when I was on earth. At one time we were very dear to each other."

Ron: "You still are to her."

Thomas: "Yes, but it was my stupidity that pulled us apart."

Ron: "But she is waiting for you now."

Thomas: "If she can ever forgive the terrible things that I have done."

Ron: "She understands that with your alcoholism, you opened yourself up to the lower forces, and it was from those lower forces that these things happened, because you were defenceless against them."

Thomas: "Well, I thought the influence of the drink would cut out all the things which I did not like at that time, but it made things much worse."

Ron: "That's right. It opened the door to let these lower beings control you. My friend you have to go on. All these things can be corrected. These things can be made good again, and you can leave behind a legacy of light to the people who will occupy this house. The darkness that you brought to this house has already cost one life, hasn't it? Not of your making, because the person had a clinical condition, and had no defence. We need to bring light into this dwelling, and you can do that by acknowledging that we all make mistakes, and by our mistakes we learn. For your comfort, I know the effect of alcohol, but I had helpful people who guided me away from alcohol - you did not have that."

Thomas: "Well, Rose, She tried."

Ron: "She tried, but she did not have the knowledge of how to bring you away from it."

Thomas: "In those days, my friend, it was the man who was in charge of the house."

Ron: "I am aware of that, but that was in the past and now you have to live by the standards that are here now."

Thomas: "I can understand that, and I think that Rose will help me from now on, and I will be by her side as she wished."

Ron: "And will you look upwards now? There are two people who want you to see them."

Thomas: "I know, especially Dad. The whole family has come and they are all trying to talk at the same time. It's twisting my brain around and around."

Ron: "They are excited. For so long the have been trying to let you know they are there."

Thomas: "So, my dear friends, if I may be permitted to call you that, I will go with my family, take the darkness and turn it into light."

Ron: "And take the help of those spirit friends who are waiting with your family. They will teach you to generate that light back into this dwelling ."

Thomas: "Yes, my friend. There is one stepping forward past Father, Mother and Rose. He is going to help me, and both of us will bring light to many other people."

Ron: "That's a good beginning. You have suffered long in the dark."

Thomas: "It will not only be my effort but a combined effort of me, my spirit friends, and people on earth."

Ron: "That is great news. It was in the early 20's that you passed. Do you know what the date is now? It is 2003."

Thomas: (Wondering) "Oh! Good gracious me."

Ron: "That is long enough for anyone to serve their time."

Thomas: "If it is all right with you, I will close my eyes and go on to the spirit world, as I should have done many years ago."
Ron: "Reach out your hand to Rose, and she will lead you."
Thomas: "I have Rose with one hand, and my spirit friend with the other."
Ron: "Go in peace. Bless you."
Thomas: "I go in peace, but also, I want to leave peace behind. I will say goodbye."

TESTIMONY

The reader may wonder how people feel after they have been relieved of the unwanted presence of a spirit. We do some research but there is not room to quote many accounts. Here is a reply to a questionnaire we sent to the couple in the above account.

CAN YOU DESCRIBE THE EVENTS THAT MADE YOU THINK SPIRITS WERE THE CAUSE OF YOUR PROBLEM?

Spirits were seen by three different people, including one sighting by two people of a child in a mirror. Things went missing and were returned days later. The culprit obviously had a mischievous sense of humour. Things in the bathroom were thrown on the floor. All the electrics in the shop were turned off. There was tremendous feeling of oppression in upstairs rooms. I personally felt terrible feelings of anxiety and panic. I had to get out of the main bedroom.

WHAT WAS THE WORST THING ABOUT THE EXPERIENCE WITH THE GHOST?

It was the sheer terror of it! The most frightening spirit was one first seen by David. It appeared as he was washing up in the kitchen. He felt there was someone behind him and, on turning round, this shimmering mass rose up from under the door. It was faceless. It then disappeared, either by going back under the door or by dissipating. There were quite a number of encounters. The temperature dropped on each occasion.

WHO WAS MOST WORRIED BY THE SPIRIT?

My husband was most affected by the Spirit. And since the house was let out to a tenant, as landlord, he had to do certain work in the house from time to time. And he would not enter the house unless he was accompanied by myself or the tenant. He certainly would not have gone there after dark.

DID THE PROBLEMS CEASE AFTER OUR VISIT?

It was amazing! David and I went in there the next day. His first

words to me were, 'It's gone!' It was just as if someone had opened a window and blown all the darkness away. It felt fresh, so different! The dark clouds had been lifted away and peace had returned.
J. & D. H.

Case 42 (R229) Haunted for Nine Years

Dawn rang me to ask for help for her daughter, Samantha, who was being mentally persecuted by the spirit of her grandfather. He had sexually abused her when she was young, and since his death, nine years ago, he had haunted them both, driving them to distraction.

We arranged to meet them at the Exeter Spiritualist Church at 7.30 pm on 13th April 2004, together with a more experienced friend who would accompany them. After welcoming them, six of us arranged ourselves in a circle in the Healing Room.

After I opened in prayer, John quickly went into a trance and our guide, Grey Cloud, spoke through him.

Grey Cloud: "Good evening to you, dear old friends. Good evening to you, ladies. You have not got the old butterflies in the tummy have you?"
Ladies: "Yes, we have."
Grey Cloud: "Tell them to go away. There is nothing to fear. I am going to step to one side for a few minutes, because I have one of my little friends who will cheer you up a bit."
Chippy: (with a strong cockney accent) "Allo governor."
Michael: "Hello Chippy."
Chippy: "My name's Chippy - all right? Now I know what you're thinking, what are you doing here? Well I'm here at the moment, but I live in the spirit world. Do you know where that is? Well it's right round you. It's 'ere now – all right?
(To a spirit) Cor, blimey. You can go away an' all mate.
(To Dawn) I'm talking to this gentleman that's stood by you, my love – all right?"
Dawn: "Yes."
Chippy: "E's a right 'andful, him, in' 'e?' 'E's come up against the wrong crowd – I'll tell you that now! (To the ladies) Are you two friends of this lady? (Samantha)"
Dawn: "I'm family, she's a friend."
Chippy: (To the friend) "You're more scared than what these two are. (She laughs and agrees) I don't know what you two got to be scared about. Do you feel better now? Good! There's nowt to worry about – and that gentleman stood by you – 'e can't hurt you. So put that thought out of your mind won't you?"

Dawn: "I will."
Chippy: "You bin trying to do it for a long time ain't you? As I said, he's come up the wrong pathway. 'E's met the wrong people, tonight, specially my boss, that's the one who spoke before. 'E's what I call the boss, so 'e's going to come back in a minute and we'll see if we can get this geezer to talk."
(To spirit) "Hah! That's what you think, mate!"
(To ladies) "So you're all right, now aren't you?"
Ladies: "Yes."
Chippy: (To Dawn) "You got to eat a lot of fruit."
Dawn: "Yes."
Chippy: "For that condition, down here?" (Pats his stomach)
Dawn: "Yes."
Chippy: (To Michael) "That's got her worried, governor, -she thinks, 'How does 'e know about that?"

    (To Dawn) "Don't worry, don't worry! Have you got connections with London, by the way?"
Dawn: "Yes."
Chippy: "I fought you 'ad. I'd better not start, or this boss 'll tell me off, and not only 'im but my boss over 'ere, 'e'll tell me off as well. I'm going to pop off for a little while and I'll come back again, afterwards. All right? My name's Chippy and I'll tell you how I come to be in the spirit world."
Grey Cloud: "Good evening, once again. I don't know if my little friend told you what my name is. My name is Grey Cloud. I have been with my friend (John) more or less since he was born, but that is not what we are here for."

    Silence
Grey Cloud: "You can't hurt me."

    Silence
Grey Cloud: "That's better. (To Ron) My dear brother, I was talking to this gentleman, do you understand?"
Ron: "Yes I know."
Grey Cloud: "He was trying to push me to one side and I had to show him who was in charge, which I am not, but all our friends on this side of life are. We just show him that the strength of love is much stronger, than what he has, or what he thinks he has. We will try to see if we can get him to say why he has taken this path."
Spirit: "I don't like being here".
Ron: "Why not?"
Spirit "For one thing it is what I am not used to. The other reason is, that in coming here, I have lost some of the power, which I had."

Ron: "It depends what you wanted the power for. Do you realize that for these mundane powers that you're referring to, there is a higher power? That is why your power had no effect. Do you realize where you have been since you have passed from this life?"

Spirit: "Not really."

Ron: "You have gone to the one place you have prepared for yourself - The Astral Plane - and it is exactly as you made it."

Spirit: "I made it grey and ugly then".

Ron: "But there is another place you could go to: it is not a place of visible power, or for indulging your own feelings. It is a place where you realize that giving is a far better way than taking. Do you know what the date was when you passed out of the physical life?"

Spirit: "Not that I can remember, my friend".

Ron: "But it was a long time ago, wasn't it?"

Spirit: "Yes".

Ron: "But all this time you have not been very happy."

Spirit: "No, it has not been, I have not been a happy person, nor made other people happy."

Ron: "You know, just in front of you, slightly to the right, there's somebody that you should know."

Spirit: "Yes, I know".

Ron: "Somebody who comes with a great deal of love, as only a mother can love a child. You did not expect to see her again."

Spirit: "No".

Ron: "Why do you think she's come? To take you to a much better place than you've been. For long years she's been trying to reach you. Every time she tries to reach you, you use that same semi-hate, I say semi-hate because even you don't like the effect."

Spirit: "No".

Ron: "But that has not deterred this lady. You have been long enough in the astral realms to want something better. Yes?"

Spirit: "Yes."

Ron: "If you will go with the Mother Lady, she will take you to a better place. Would you like to do that?"

Spirit: "I will. Yes of course."

Ron: "One thing you will have to do. You will have to make some retribution for the unhappiness you have caused to another person here."

Spirit: "Yes! How can I find the words to put this behind me? The words I want to say, don't come to me. If you could ever find it within your heart, to give forgiveness for what pain I have caused you and others within the family. But, my friends I would ask forgiveness from the bottom of my heart, in

the presence of all these people gathered round to watch and to give me strength to go forward from now on. I do give you my promise, here and now, that all your troubles that I have caused, will cease."
Michael: "Well done."
Spirit: "You will be able to sleep and not worry if anything will happen, it will not be me."
Ron: "Do you know Albert?"
Spirit: "I know Albert. He's over this side as well."
Ron: "He's come down to give you strength to go forward."
Spirit: "He's here with my -----. How is it that I find it very difficult to say 'Mother'?"
Ron: "She does not find it difficult to say 'son". If you will go and take her hand and travel to a higher level - but there is no going back"
Spirit: "No! I know. Your friend, and the friend of our brother, is looking at me, as if to say, 'Well if you do, you've had it!"
Ron: "Go in peace, go in love."
Spirit: "I will, and I will leave behind me, as I travel forwards with my friends, I will leave love with our friends here and the other one as well. I must thank you for giving support to the lady. You were not going mad. It was only the thoughts that I was putting into your mind. They will cease. There's no need for them now. So I am going onward and upward with the two friends I have here."
Chippy: "Hello Governor."
Michael: "Are you going to tell us something?"
Chippy: "Of course I am. I promised the lady. I promised to tell her how I came into the spirit world. You know this last war don't yer?"
Dawn: "Yes."
Chippy: "Well you know the old 'Buzz Bombs'?"
Dawn: "Yes".
Chippy: "I wun't killed by a buzz bomb. I was going up the street and there was a shop that was hit, you see, and there was some children in there. I popped in, got two of them out and when I went back for the other one, the building collapsed on me. That's all I can remember."
Michael "Were you a carpenter, Chippy?"
Chippy: "No, I wasn't a carpenter – I was called Carpenter, that's why they called me Chippy.
(To Samantha) You all right now, love?"
Samantha: "Yes."
Chippy: "And the other two ladies?"
Ladies: "Yes, thank you."
Chippy: (to the friend) "You get trouble with your foot?"

Friend: "I do, yes."

Chippy: "Why don't you go to the ole foot doctor? Too dear, she's going to say – I just put that in to give you the ole 'cheery up bit'. The boss is telling me, 'Come on you – 'op it, so I better go. Let me leave you with the love of Spirit, the love of all your friends who are over this side. Rest assured that everything is going to be all right from now on. God bless you. I don't need to say God bless you to him and him. They knows what I fink."

Grey Cloud: "My dear brothers I hope you did not mind our little friend coming through?"

Michael: "No, we enjoyed it."

Grey Cloud: "He is a little rascal, but it is what he wanted to do, cheer people up, because the lady has been carrying a burden on her shoulders for so long.

(to Samantha) It has been wearing you down – very much. Now you can say to that worry, 'Hop it! Have a strong mind. If you feel any unpleasantness, just close your eyes and say, 'Please go away'. If it stays, put it in your prayers in the name of Grey Cloud.

I will say, God bless you, good night."

All: "Goodnight."

WHAT DO PEOPLE DO IN THE SPIRIT WORLD?
CHAPTER 15

Any reader who is new to this idea of life continuing after death, may reasonably ask, what do these people do, after they are rescued. What do they do, and how do they spend their time in this Spirit World? The answer is that they do whatever attracts them on the level they are at. This means that there is an enormous variety of occupations. My sister-in-law, who was a very devout member of the Church of England, and was never interested in my version of life after death, came back to me to say,

"I had no idea so much went on over here. I wish I had listened when you tried to tell me about it." To illustrate just one man's description of his life after death, a man who was well known to the circle when he was alive, I describe the life of a rather high living bank manager.

A Bank Manager Goes Over.

Mr. A. said, that as a Bank Manager in Central London, he had become accustomed to being wined and dined by sycophantic people who hoped to borrow money. Because of this he had become rather grandiose and self-important and he was reluctant to leave earth surroundings. He had a feeling that in the astral or spirit realm, there would be no deception - he would be seen for exactly what he was, smug and self-satisfied. He also felt he might have to judge himself, as well, and so he put the whole thing off for a bit.

In doing this, he said he was a bit of a naughty boy, but he found out some very interesting things. As a Bank Manager he had always been interested in economics, the science of money. Now that he was invisible to most earthly eyes, he could attend economic conferences, the well known, ones and the secret ones, which the public never hear about, and he could see for himself how great business houses influence politics and newspapers, and determine the fate of individuals and even nations. All this turned out to be useful knowledge later on, when he had learned to change his attitude from selfishness, to one of wanting to help mankind. He then took on the task of attending such conferences to try and influence powerful people, so as to increase human welfare and avoid unnecessary wars.

When Mr. A. came through the medium to speak in the circle, he had been in spirit for nearly fifty years, and he had learned a great deal. He found that even Bank Managers, can be useful in the Spirit World. Once he had adjusted to the new life, and realised that service to others is the coin of the Spirit, he started to meet other Bank Managers as they came over, to explain to them what had happened to them and what this new world was like.

He did say that he found it rather unpleasant at first in Spirit, because he had never learned to control his lower emotions and desires, and he found these were shown in his aura to everyone he met. In time he learned to control these, and, as he got used to the new life, he felt more comfortable.

He was asked about relaxation and pleasures he enjoyed after spells of working. He said it was just as well he had not been asked that question fifty years ago or they'd have been shocked by the answer.

He said he had never been very fond of gardening but as a church organist he had always been interested in music and he had been able to develop this. He had always enjoyed musical concerts and he said that these were simply wonderful in the Spirit World. All music there had colour coming from the players as they played, so that you saw wonderful colours rising and blending as you listened. Then when the audience was stirred by the music, colours rose from them as well, making a brilliant ever-changing vista of colours, some of which could never been seen on earth. These colours go back to the players who feel the audience's pleasure, and and this colour fills the whole auditorium. He said that even the finest symphonies on earth were only copies of originals in the spirit world, which had been transmitted to their composers, and only in spirit could one hear the perfection of music. He said that Beethoven's Ninth, with an enormous choir, was the most wonderful musical experience he had ever had. He had now learned to play two more instruments and had a group of musical friends who all enjoyed playing sessions together.

'Did he continue with his wining and dining?' he was asked. When he first settled down in spirit, he did indulge in eating and drinking, as he had been accustomed to do on earth. He had quite given this up now, as there was no need - all nourishment came from the ether. He did say, however, that those who have known physical love of their partners on earth have no idea of the joy and ecstasy of true love in the spirit world, where spirits who are completely in tune can actually merge completely with one another in mutual love.

He said that looking back to earth, after the colour and beauty of the Spirit World, all seemed dark and ugly, except where the evolution of love and forgiveness causes light to shine from someone's heart, because in the spirit world, everyone has a radiance, which shows their whole nature. When he sees earth people, he similarly looks for the light they emit. Sadly, some have very little at all, some show the red flame of material desire or strength of will, and others only appear as shadows because of ill health.

Mr. A. said that although on earth he had enjoyed some power, wealth and good living, it all seemed very poor in retrospect, compared with the colour, gaiety, comradeship and love to be found in Spirit. Above all, he said, as you progress in Spirit you feel an inexpressible joy in life, which makes earthly pleasures pale by comparison.

It was interesting that throughout his talk, Mr A. carefully avoided the question of who his present companion was, and he asked his son not to enquire about it. It is said that where married couples are not really in tune in this life, on passing they naturally gravitate to those with whom they are in tune and with whom they feel most comfortable.

So, although by some standards, our Bank Manager was not an ideal character during his earthly life, and although he was at first a reluctant learner in the world of spirit, it appears that after some initial discomfort, he became both useful and contented, as he experienced the richness and beauty of the love and life in the spirit world - the world to which each of us, in turn, must one day make our way.

What Do Children Do in the Spirit World?

Children are cared for by relatives, or by helpers, who have chosen to do this work because of their love of children. In the book, 'Billy Grows up in Spirit,' Billy describes in great detail how at first everything he wanted for fun was provided, and then it all disappeared, and he was told he now had to learn how to make things by the power of thought. After some hilarious attempts, he managed to make a football, because it was something he was familiar with. He had to go to school, which he said was much better than schools on earth, where he used to muck about and flick pellets. Three members of our group are earthly teachers and we had to agree with him about this.

After school he went on to college and then the equivalent of a university and eventually he was chosen to do rescue work himself, under the guidance of supervisors, which involved quite a long period where he studied the person to be helped before he tried to intervene. Billy had plenty of fun and games with other young people and was very pleased when tapes of his talks went to interested people around the world.

Provided they have not become lost, because some trauma, or wrong teaching, has temporarily held them up, children find the new world exciting, even enthralling, once they have got over their natural grief at missing their families.

IS THERE ANY PROOF?

Having been one of the sceptics about a life after death, I well understand the reasonable demand for proof of the reality of Rescue Work. As the great scientist, Einstein, said about feeling, 'Cosmic Consciousness,'

"It's very hard to convince anyone who has not had the same experience." Obviously, for me, the events described in this book are my proof. To sit regularly with our team of mediums, as I do, to hear the spirits telling their story, and to see a mediums face change in front of me, from deep despair to hope, and finally, to delight, is a constant reinforcement of the fact that we really are able to help these lost souls. Then, again, the fact that I have over seven hundred recordings to refer to when I want to refresh my memory of a session, confirms their reality for me.

The fact that, after her death, Nancy advised me to remarry and then congratulated me on making the right choice of partner, just as Charlie did to Lily, is a very real proof to both of us, of the reality of communications from the 'so called,' dead. The fact that both Charlie and Nancy communicate with us almost weekly, giving us advice on medical and veterinary matters, as well as telling me to have the brakes or the exhaust checked on the car, is further proof to us that they still know many details about our daily life.

But what evidence would a hardened sceptic accept? Financial evidence, perhaps? A visit, to a household that has been freed from an entity? Most people wish to keep their sufferings and their subsequent relief to them selves, but there are one or two who might be willing for the affair to be made public.

When we visit houses where a family has been upset, even terrified, by a spirit or ghost, we only charge for our petrol, for we see our work as a form of service. However, when offered, we will accept a donation towards church funds. It is when we have, in collaboration with our guides, moved a spirit on, and a month later we receive a donation of from £10 to £50, together with a letter of thanks for peace restored, that we have some evidence that a sceptic might accept. This does show up in the annual church accounts.

We do know of people who do this work professionally. They charge £300 down and £50 an hour for the work, and find employment with property companies when activity hold up the sale, or letting, of expensive properties. Unfortunately, these charges put these services beyond the reach of many people, no matter what distress they are in.

On passing from this life, which we all have to do eventually, every one finds that life, and full awareness, continues. The object of this book is to help people escape the possible troubles, and enjoy to the full, this life that awaits us all. You, dear reader, are a soul, and you cannot die. The 20th Century myth that there is no life after death must finally be exposed for what it is – a myth with no foundation in fact.

What Does Science Say?

At the moment, most scientists still believe that consciousness depends on the physical brain. My feeling is, that there is no evidence for this belief, and therefore it must be based on an instinctive feeling, perhaps, that that they prefer to deal with matters that can be investigated in the laboratory. One cannot say that it is a materialist idea for Einstein has shown us that matter is only a form of energy. If their belief is correct, when the brain disintegrates at death, most scientists conclude that all consciousness ceases, and therefore there can be no life after death.

Many individual scientists do have a faith, are Christians, Buddhists or Hindus, perhaps, and they do believe in an afterlife. Some of the greatest scientists and inventors have believed in a life after death and have communicated with people who have passed from this life, but, from a professional point of view it will do a scientist no good at the moment, to publish such views. Even to suggest that there is a power unknown to science by which mind can influence another mind at a distance or influence matter, is heresy. When Professor Jahn, Dean in the Science Department of Princeton University, devised a machine which clearly showed that it could be inflenced by thought alone, he was dismissed from his post as Dean.

The Spiritualist, Sir William Crookes, who was President of the Royal Society and also President of most of the other scientific bodies of his day, made many discoveries that affect us to this day. He invented the first sunglasses to protect our eyes, discovered the metal Thallium, the Cathode Ray Tube, the screen on which we watch our televisions, and improved our modern sanitation systems. He recorded hundreds of experiments with a medium he had staying in his house for long periods, which completely convinced him of the truth of survival of the human spirit, yet he was vilified for holding such views. Just before his death he said he was still completely sure that his views were correct.

Logie Baird, who invented the first television system used by the BBC, the first colour television, the first experimental 3D television, and the infrared camera, was convinced of the survival of death and actually received a message in Morse code, from the dead Thomas Edison, the great American inventor. Edison started working life as a telegraph boy on the American railways and was a skilled telegraph operator. He had tried to devise a machine capable of contacting the next world but failed. He was the most prolific inventor the world has ever seen, having over a thousand patents for his discoveries, but the development of electrical power and lighting was his greatest, transforming the modern world, where modern factories are based on the use of the power that he developed and our houses are lit by electric light he pioneered. On the centenary of his death, all the public lights in America were switched off and on again in memory of his work.

Sir Oliver Lodge, was Professor of Physics at Liverpool University, and the first Principal of Birmingham University. He developed the first successful transmission and reception of radio signals and sold his patent to Marconi. With his sons he developed the sparking plug on which most of our car engines rely to this day. Sir Oliver Lodge was a convinced Spiritualist and the family regularly heard from his son, Raymond, who perished in the Great War. The book 'Raymond,' that told of the communications from his dead son, was a best seller. These scientific spiritualists have literally transformed our modern world.

Alfred Russell Wallace was a famous naturalist who, independently of Darwin, conceived the idea of Evolution or the Origin of Species through Natural Selection. He wrote to Darwin and they published their first paper together, in 1858, which caused outrage in the religious world, but these ideas are almost universally accepted today. He was an outspoken Spiritualist, and he came through to speak to us in our group on the very day I borrowed his book, 'Miracles and Modern Spiritualism,' from the public library.

Little Billy, in the book, 'Billy Grows Up in Spirit,' states that many scientists who pass over, continue with their work, and when humanity is thought fit to make good use of them, inventions are passed down to scientists who are capable of grasping them, by telepathy or in dreams.

My own conclusion, for what it is worth, is that all scientists will find the truth when they pass at death. I look forward to the day when they find it while they are still living. After watching the mediums John Edward and James Van Praagh, demonstrating on television, I wrote a little poem and sent it to the New Scientist magazine. They praised it but did not publish it.

PASSING ON
When you've heard from your mother,
Your father and your brother,
Although they've all been dead for many years.
And they seem fully fit,
And their wisdom and their wit
Is better than it was in later years.
It causes one to doubt,
What scientists are about,
When they say that the mind is just the brain,
For it has been demonstrated

>That the brain has been negated,
>For all were cremated,
>Each the same.
>There's no one in the radio,
>Although it sings a song.
>There's no one in the vidio,
>But if it should go wrong,
>The Tape is still OK.
>The mind is not the brain,
>Which gravitates to earth,
>The self is still the same,
>And death is just rebirth.

I greatly admire the discoveries of modern science and love to read of them. The pace of discovery speeds up every year and we learn more and more of the secrets of nature. I think most scientists would admit that in a thousand years time, our present level of knowledge will have been far surpassed. In ten thousand years, our present knowledge will seem quite primitive, compared to the level reached by then, so the verdict of science is not, and never can be final on this or any other matter. There is always more to be discovered.

Let me finish with two quotations:

"We are at a turning point in our understanding of our minds and nature."
Rupert Sheldrake Ph.D.

About the book by Dean Radin Ph.D., 'The Conscious Universe.'
"Cutting perceptively through the spurious arguments frequently made by sceptics, (Radin) shows the evidence in favour of paranormal existence is overwhelming."
Brian Josephson, Nobel Laureate in Physics and Professor of Physics, Cambridge University.

CONCLUSIONS The evidence we have found in doing Rescue Work has shown us that knowledge of what really happens after death is important for every one, regardless of where they live on the planet. While most people are reunited with friends and loved ones, quite a large number find them selves stuck in a kind of limbo, sometimes for many years. To avoid this unnecessary distress after death, everyone needs to know about the things that caused our clients to need rescuing. These are the main causes we have found:

(a) Having a firm belief that there is no life after death - that death is the end! Mark, the Skier and the lady in,'Walking, Walking, Walking,' are examples of this.
(b) Having a firm belief that, after death, one will lie in the grave until the Last Trump at the end of the world. Fortescue, and, The Girl in the Box, are examples of this.
(c) A guilty conscience, combined with a fear of Hell, can cause a spirit to fight against going on towards the light. Wilf, is one of many examples of this.
(d) Being bewildered at finding themselves still alive and conscious after death, a spirit may take refuge in a favorite house or other building. or even a person. This happened to many of the spirits mentioned in the section on Hauntings.

Because the spiritual level achieved on earth will automatically take a person among people of the same level in the spirit world, evil people will find themselves surrounded by other evil people, in a very grim world, as Wilf did. Only when they, themselves, wish to improve, will the watching helpers be able to start to help them, in some cases, bringing them to a rescue circle on earth.

THE CURSE OF IGNORANCE

The common factor in all these cases is ignorance - ignorance of the truth about the afterlife. The object of this book is to tell people the truth, so that, in Conan Doyle's words, "People do not come over here to dwell in darkness."

If, after your death, you find yourself going through a tunnel towards a light, have no fear. Soon loved ones and helpers will appear and all will be well. If, after death, you find yourself stuck in what appears to be an unpleasant dream, ask for help from a loved one or friend who has already passed. If, at first, they seem to be slow in coming, call on a favourite pet who has passed – we have never known this to fail – and they will lead you to a loved one, friend or helper. Keep your mind as steady as you can. In this new world, to think intensely of a person or a place, will take you there very quickly. When Indira Gandhi returned after her assassination, she was all over the place until she was told, 'Go to Nehru! - her father - which settled her down.

Be assured, this new world can be happier and more beautiful than you dared to hope. As Raynor Johnson and many others have said, "It is better than I thought it could possibly be". After his death, a friend, Professsor Wilson Knight, came through to me to say, "Michael, it's better that we hoped!"

At first your friends and loved ones will show themselves as you last remember seeing them. Later they will appear as they really are at the time – in the prime of life. You, too, will revert to that happy stage of life, where you combined health with experience and were free of the pains and handicaps of an aging body.

WHAT SHOULD WE TEACH CHILDREN

I think that what people tell children about a life after death depends on two things. Firstly, what they themselves believe to be true, and secondly, what they think it best for children to know at their particular age.

In view of our discoveries in talking to dead people, and giving them guidance, I would suggest that above all, children should not be given a frightening view of death, nor should they think it means oblivion – ceasing to exist. When an elderly relative dies, the attitude could be, "Oh, well, they'll be happy now! They'll be with so and so, and so and so." Let children have the idea, which is the truth, that the real person, the soul, moves on to a new life, leaving behind their physical body, and that they will have a new spiritual body, as will all those they know who have already passed over. This knowledge may one day, save him or her from the distressing situation some of our clients find themselves in.

As children grow older, the idea could be introduced that the quality of life after death, depends on how the person has acted in this life; whether they have treated other people, and creatures, with respect and kindness.

Let children know that those who loved them in life, will still love them after death, and will still try to help them in their difficulties, while bearing in mind that we all grow by solving our own problems, as far as we can. A sceptical friend of mine, a film producer, lent his son his deceased grandfather's pen, to use in an entrance examination for the Royal Navy. To his surprise, the boy told him, afterwards, that he was sure his grandfather, an ex-naval officer, had helped him to answer a difficult question in the examination.

Most of the above suggestions can be made in the context of the major religions, which all teach the existence of a life of some kind after death.

Perhaps some of my readers will be kind enough to contact me when we are all over there, to discuss my ideas and, perhaps, to correct them. One of my pupils has already come back to say I did not get it quite right when I taught in school; he died at 17 in a motor-cycle accident. No two cases are ever quite the same, as we shall all find out in due course.

For Further Reading.
Holy Ghostbuster, by Rev.J. Aelwyn Roberts
Soul Rescuers, a 21st Century Guide to the Spirit World,
by Terry & Natalie O'Sullivan
Wounded Spirits, by Dr Leslie Weatherhead, former
President, of the Methodist Church.
Crossing Over, by John Edward
Heaven and Earth, by James Van Praagh
Ghosts and Earthbound Spirits by Linda Williamson
Billy Grows Up in Spirit by Michael Evans.
(£5.00 incl. P&P from 01392 438434)
(Some copies of the original recordings of spirits talking are available for a limited period from 01392 438434)

The End   © Copyright by Michael Evans, 2007

Due to illnes the 'Ghost Hunting' trio ceased operations in September 2006. The rescue circle continues.